MAKING MAVERICKS

FROSTY HESSON WITH IAN SPIEGELMAN

SKYHORSE PUBLISHING

Skyhorse Publishing books may be purchased in bulk at special discounts for sales promotion, corporate gifts, fund-raising, or educational purposes. Special editions can also be created to specifications. For details, contact the Special Sales Department, Skyhorse Publishing, 307 West 36th Street, 11th Floor, New York, NY 10018 or info@skyhorsepublishing.com.

Skyhorse® and Skyhorse Publishing® are registered trademarks of Skyhorse Publishing, Inc.®, a Delaware corporation.

Visit our website at www.skyhorsepublishing.com.

10 9 8 7 6 5 4 3 2 1

Library of Congress Cataloging-in-Publication Data is available on file.

ISBN: 978-1-62087-875-0

Printed in the United States of America

CONTENTS

PROLOGUE

I had been coaching Jay Moriarity for four years when his whole world changed on a fifty-foot monster of a wave that almost killed him. Instead, it made him famous.

At just sixteen, he was by far the youngest surfer to take on Mavericks, a reef break half a mile off the California coast at Half Moon Bay that at the time was recognized as having some of the largest waves anywhere in the world. Some of the most legit surfers in the game had even conceded that when Mavs was on, it was more powerful than the legendary waves at Waimea on the North Shore of Oahu—and that had been considered the all-time mecca of big wave surfing since the late 1950s. So for a kid Jay's age to surf Mavericks was unheard of.

To say that Mavericks isn't for kids is doing it an injustice. It's hardly for *people*. I'd been surfing it for seven years when Jay had his life-altering moment. I had seen world-renowned, big-wave riders paddle out and look at the building-sized, dark green wall of ocean rushing at them with such incredible force that the water actually gets sucked backward up the face of the wave. Most of them turned around and went home. These were people who'd conquered breaks all over the globe, but they simply wanted nothing to do with Mavs.

Jay, though, he wanted to slay dragons.

As a coach I'd worked with dozens and dozens of young people, training them toward the goal of not merely being the best athletes they could be, but more importantly the best *people* they could be—respectful, responsible, passionate human beings. But when Jay, as a scrawny twelve year old who'd somehow gotten up the nerve to come over to my van at Pleasure Point in Santa Cruz, asked me to teach him about surfing, his enthusiasm for learning what I had to offer totally blew me away. He had a vision of who he wanted to be and the ceaseless determination to make it happen—you could see it in his bright blue eyes and the killer grin that drew everyone to him.

If not for his passion and eagerness to do the work, I would never have let the kid anywhere near Mavericks. We'd been working together on basic technique and then contest surfing for two and a half years before he even brought it up. After that the real work began, and it was another year and a half before I let him paddle out at Half Moon Bay.

He hadn't even been surfing Mavs a whole season when the wipeout happened.

A photographer caught it on camera. A week later the photo was in *The New York Times*. A month after that it was on the cover of *Surfer* magazine, and to this day it's still one of the most famous surf shots ever taken. Like I said, the wave could have killed Jay, but his training had pulled him through, and it really was a beautiful photo. So we threw a party.

Boots McGhee and his wife Carm decided to host it at their house on the beach flats at Aptos. Everyone was invited. They must have had seventy-five people jammed into their living room and dining room and another hundred outside. The Santa Cruz surfing community really *is* a community. Jay belonged to a club called Big Stick Surfing Association, which was a group of long-boarders, and I belonged to the Santa Cruz Long Board Union. Both clubs put on non-profit surf contests that gave money to the Junior Lifeguards and the Santa Cruz Surf Museum; they established scholarship funds for kids in the neighborhood, bought equipment for the lifeguards, and just generally fulfilled a number of community-based support needs. Around here, that's the way it's done.

Bob Barbour, the photographer who snapped the now-famous shot was there, along with Jay's mom, Christy, and his girlfriend, Kim. And, of course, Jay's surf buddies were partying with him—Shylo Steinthal, Bobby Brown, Mikey DiGregorio, Neil "Moose" Matthies, Steve Thomas, and Jed Noll, whose dad, Greg Noll, is the grandfather of big wave surfing and a Waimea legend.

It was a whole scene. Everybody was all stoked and everybody was so psyched for Jay. It was party *on*, totally a great time. Boots's people were musicians—his dad was a very famous jazz man from back in the forties—and Carm's people were from the Philippines, so that combo means there was a lot of great music and a lot of great food.

There was chicken fixed a couple of different ways, short ribs, and there was a keg or two because we're surfers, you know, and we don't have any money. There were sodas for the junior members, potato salad, macaroni salad, green salads. It was lightweight in the sense that we weren't roasting a pig—it wasn't a Hawaiian hukilau. Everybody brought a little something to be able to have a big function without tapping anybody too much.

Everybody was just having a blast. When my wife Brenda and I showed up, right away Jay and I started laughing and joking and there were congratulations all the way around. Since the party was at Boots's house he was playing emcee, directing the festivities, and finally he decided to publicly acknowledge why we were all there. He went into a little speech about how he enjoyed our community and how its support had led to Jay's success, how that success had landed Bob Barbour's photo in *The New York Times*—that was a big deal for us. Plus, the magazine cover acknowledged that Mavericks was a legit, world-class surf spot. Boots just wanted to give three cheers for Jay. We all did.

When the speech was done, I let the room settle down a bit, and then I said, "Well, I would like to follow that up with a little something. Thank you to everyone for being here. Thank you to our hosts Boots and Carm for opening up their house for all of this to happen, and it truly does take a community."

At that point, Brenda went out to the car and brought back the gift-wrapped surprise I had gotten for Jay, and I continued: "All of you know who I am and everybody has a certain perception of me. It has come to my attention that among the kids that I have worked with there's a joke that still persists about some of my accomplishments and endeavors—and that there's a mention of a wheelbarrow and the suggestion that I use it to carry around a particular part of my anatomy…"

I passed over the present to Jay and everybody was cheering. Jay and I made eye contact. He's got his little smirking smile and I've got mine. It was like, "Here we are, here's the deal, here it is—doors are opening for you."

So he undoes the ribbon and takes off the wrapping paper in one motion. And there is this gold-painted toy wheelbarrow that is probably a foot long and seven inches wide, with two little handles and just one wheel on it.

Everybody started cracking up and Jay gave me his "are-you-kidding-me?" look. I just smiled and told him, "If you continue on the path that you've begun, then you can earn your way up into a larger wheelbarrow. Mine doesn't fit in the car."

He came over laughing, gave me a big hug, then he looked at me and caught me completely off-guard by saying, "I have something for you, too."

Turning to the crowd, he said, "Everybody knows how important Frosty has been. All of the time we have worked together and been together, you guys only know a small portion of what was really going on and how much he has truly meant to me. So, Frosty, I have something to give to you."

He handed over a gift-wrapped present. I said thanks and gave him another hug, holding up the present for everybody to see because it was so nicely wrapped. Then I carefully took the paper off. There was a plaque inside. The inscription read:

Frosty,
You've been my inspiration.
Thank you for your continual guidance and support.
Love, Jay.
February 25th, 1995

Tears came to my eyes. There were still so many things I had to teach that kid. How to be a good human being wasn't one of them.

PART I
I WANT TO GO *THERE*

CHAPTER ONE

Before I ever got near a wave, never mind a wave the size of Mavericks, my parents were already worried about the kind of trouble I could get into if there was water around. We were living in San Francisco in the early 1950s, there was still a lot of untouched wilderness to be explored, and my parents wanted to experience as much of it as they could. The only problem was that by the time I was three, if I caught sight of a lake, a stream, or a creek, I'd go and jump right in before anyone could stop me. It was totally cool.

Somehow my parents didn't see it that way.

Water and I just got along. I was always attracted to it. It didn't matter where we were. If there was a swimming hole, if there was something to get into water-wise, I was there, I was *in*. My parents were concerned, because they loved going to the ocean and they were afraid that I'd jump in that, too, if I ever got a chance.

"Richard has no fear of water," my mother told a friend who was a lifeguard at the Crystal Plunge and Sutro Baths.

The Sutro Baths were a series of heated, indoor pools on a cliff above the ocean just north of the Cliff House in San Francisco. All it is now is a bunch of deserted concrete areas—there's no superstructure left, no way of knowing what it used to be, but it was the happening spot in the Bay Area at the time. Community pools were a big part of the region's post-war housing boom, so along with the Crystal Plunge there were also the Hayward Plunge and the Santa Cruz Plunge. The Plunges were a point of civic pride, with the pools housed in buildings shaped like enormous Quonset huts with steel roofs, three concrete walls, and one wall that was floor-to-ceiling glass so that the sunlight could flood in and sparkle on the water.

Like a lot of the Plunge lifeguards, my mother's friend was a water clown. Water clowns would put on these amazing displays of diving, swimming, and water acrobatics, and the whole neighborhood would come to watch. So these were experienced, qualified people, and this guy was a very famous lifeguard in San Francisco. In the early fifties nobody really taught their kids to swim until they were significantly older than I was, but my parents were very worried about me, so they thought that if this guy could instill a fear of water in me, it would slow me down, and they wouldn't have to worry quite as much.

It was important to them that they were having me checked out by a professional. That was the first life lesson they inadvertently taught me: *To become a capable, competent individual, learn from capable, competent individuals.*

When they brought me to the Plunge one spring evening when I was three, their friend took a look at me and assured them, "Oh, don't worry. Everybody has a fear of water. We just need to find his."

My mom and dad were sitting in the stands behind a short turquoise wall while I got into the shallow end with this guy and started playing and splashing around and having a good time. I remember looking back at my parents, and the guy saying to me, "What would you like to do?"

I said, "I wanna go there," and pointed to the deep end of the pool.

"Well, okay," he said. "Then go."

At first, I could walk. Then as it got deeper I started bouncing off the bottom and coming up to get a breath of air. Since I didn't know how to swim or even kick, that breath of air became harder and harder to come by as the water got deeper and deeper. Finally, the lifeguard reached down and pulled me up by the hair.

He asked me again: "What would you like to do? Where do you want to go?"

I just kept pointing to the deep end and saying, "I wanna go there!"

So he let go. I sank, I bounced back up, and I kept flailing around trying to get to the top until he grabbed me by the hair again, asking, "Where do you want to go?"

I didn't know what this guy's issue was; I'd already *told* him twice. There was just something about that deep end. The shallow end was little, for little kids. But the deep end was darker, bigger—it was *there*.

I can remember going through the sinking and bouncing process another two or three times with the guy before he finally scooped me up and took me back to the shallow end. That was not cool. I kept pointing and insisting, "No! I wanna go there!" until he gave in and swam me down to the deep end of the pool and let me touch the wall.

Then he picked me up, put me on the deck, and told my parents, "You're going to have a problem with this one. Because this kid doesn't have any fear of water in him."

He offered to help teach me how to swim.

Real swimming was going to take a while, but by the time summer rolled around I was at least proficient underwater. Being underwater just opened up a whole new world. First of all, nobody knew where I was, because a lot of the places where we swam had cloudy water, so there was this new feeling of freedom that—just for a few seconds—nobody could see me and nobody could tell me what to do. On top of that there was the freedom of being able to defy gravity, to glide up and down beneath the surface, flipping and spinning, doing anything I wanted.

It all gave me an amazing taste of independence. I got to liking it so much that I worked on staying under longer and longer, learning how to hold my breath and counting off the seconds in my head. Before I knew it, I could hold my breath for a long, long time.

Once when my mom was giving me a bath, I asked her, "How long can somebody hold their breath?"

She said, "Oh, maybe for a minute."

"But I can hold my breath for longer than that."

"No," she said, "you must be counting wrong."

I made her time me. She said her watch must be fast.

I don't think she was trying to discourage me. It was just that the science of the day dictated that people couldn't hold their breath for more than a minute before they were in real danger of drowning. So, in my mother's mind, it was impossible that a little guy my age had just held his breath for longer than a minute—it just couldn't have happened. I didn't realize then how valuable this supposedly impossible ability was going to be for me later in life, but that experience planted a seed and taught me something else: *Some people will always tell you that what you are trying to accomplish is impossible; those people have no idea what they're talking about.*

My cousins and their friends would come to this little beach called Coyote Point just south of San Francisco. We had moved to a new housing development in Hayward, across the bay from

San Francisco, by then, but my mom would drive across the Hayward/San Mateo Bridge to Coyote Point to hang out with her girlfriends. I still couldn't *swim* swim, but I could go underwater for quite a distance, and I had a blast sneaking up on the older girls because they'd just scream and become completely unglued. It was the best—getting an older kid to freak out.

Coyote Point was beautiful. My mom was a redhead, so she had to wrap herself up in blankets to keep the sun off her, but she still loved being near the water and reading her books. And Mom especially liked taking me to Coyote Point because it's a shallow beach inside San Francisco Bay with no reef breaks or shore breaks to produce any real waves. However, it wasn't long before I found out what I'd been missing.

One day, we were driving along the coast on Highway 1 between San Francisco and Santa Cruz when my parents decided to stop and hang out on the beach. It was a foggy, miserable day— as it oftentimes is near San Francisco. There was a little river that ran through the beach and into the ocean. I was in my Levi's and a T-shirt, and as soon as I saw the river I knew that I was going swimming, whether I had anything to swim in or not. So I just kicked off my sneakers and jumped in the river with my clothes on.

Of course my mom was like, "How can you *do* that?"

My dad told her, "Don't worry, he's already wet. He'll get cold and come out."

Well, I did come out. Then I headed for the ocean.

The waves were breaking way out off shore, but the whitewater that rushed over where I was wading had enough energy in it to knock me over and tumble me toward the beach. The thrill of being picked up and dumped into the soft, spraying foam and rolled up onto the sand was like being on a rollercoaster that breathed—it was motion and speed and it was alive.

It was a whole new water experience, to suddenly lose the control that I had in the river, the Bay, and the pool. Just the exhilaration of being moved around was like, *Oh, yeah!* I'd go in and then just stand up and get carried back and tossed out again. I remember my mom being pissed at my dad for letting me do it. Apparently, I stayed in so long I turned blue. Mom wrapped me up and tried to get me warm. My little teeth were chattering, but it was so worth it.

From that moment on, I wanted to go where the waves were. I wanted to go *there*.

*   *   *

As I racked up a few more summers I started being able to do things on my own and with my friends. In fact, the rule in our house was, "Get outside." After dark you could come in and watch a little TV, but there was absolutely no such thing as hanging around the house during the day. We would ride our bikes, play baseball, run around in the tall grass of the cow pastures that surrounded the neighborhood, or chase fish in the streams that ran through foothills beyond the pastures. The only parental interference we would get all day came from Hunt's canning factory. You could hear its steam whistle from anywhere in town. The noon whistle meant get home for lunch, and the 5:00 p.m. whistle was dinner. After that, sundown told us to get home for the night.

On my little adventures out into the foothills of Hayward, I would go exploring on my bike up to the streams and creeks and wherever else water would flow. I'd hang out under the oak trees and in the sun-spotted warm areas, just watching the water move. Depending on the season, there were pollywogs and frogs and all sorts of fish to check out. I was never supposed to go that far from home by myself, but my independent streak kept growing, and something was drawing me deeper and deeper into those hills.

The pastures were allowed, though, and I remember my mother walking out to them with me one spring afternoon when I was six or seven.

Some of the grasses were over four feet tall, and as kids we used to crawl around and create little trails in the grass where the adults would never see us. We had this whole network of them going all over the pastures and, to my mind, they were just for us kids.

My mom and I were walking through the shorter grasses together, talking and having a groovy time, when she stopped and said, "Come on over here."

I followed her into the tall grass and she lay down like she was going to make snow angels.

"Look up at the sky," she said, "and tell me what you see."

I lay down and looked. "Well, it's sunny and there's a bunch of clouds in the sky."

"What do the clouds look like?"

I'd never really taken a look at clouds before, so I just said, "Well, they're clouds."

"No," my mother said. "*Look* at them."

So I looked. And I began to see the different shapes. Basking under the sun in the warm grass, I saw blue sky and mixed gray and white clouds changing up there. Within a few minutes, my imagination began to drift and I saw that the clouds could be whatever I wanted them to be. There was a heart shape with a little bit of red in it and then it was a prehistoric wild boar, and then the wind blew that into the form of a shark. Just pausing to look up and watch the clouds morph, taking the time to soak it in, was magic.

I was so glad my mother taught me that. *Sometimes you need to stop what you're doing, breathe, and take the time to look around to see what's really going on.*

*   *   *

That same summer, my parents took us on vacation to the Mohave Desert. There's a ghost town there called Calico that dates back to the late 1800s, which is a long time in California history. My mom was interested in that sort of thing. I wasn't. But I came across something amazing in that abandoned mining town that grabbed hold of my imagination.

One of the miners had built a house out of wine bottles and mortar. The exterior walls were all brown, green, and clear glass, refracting and dimming the light when I stepped inside. As little kid looking at this, I was so impressed by the idea that somebody could look at something that no one else wanted, somebody else's trash, and then build something wonderful out of it. They hadn't seen garbage, but building blocks, and then a home—and it was a really *cool* home.

It was just four walls and a brownish-gray weatherboard door, the grain raised from all the moisture being sucked from the wood by the heat, but when I stood staring through those walls long enough, they became the stained glass windows of a church, and then they became a kaleidoscope. The old, timeworn bottles were laid on their sides to take the place of bricks, and the sloppy mortar work between them made them even more opaque, but it was a bright sunny day in the desert and I was fascinated by the way the curve of the bottles distorted the light filtering through them. I could see the dark shadows of people moving by, but not real people. By alternating colors, I could create little pieces of art in my imagination. There were stars and crosses and abstract forms. Maybe it was primitive art, but it was art.

Whoever had done it, they had looked at things differently. I didn't know the word "perspective," but I got the concept as soon as the light twisted through the bottles and hit my eyes. The person who made that house had taken reality and tweaked it a bit. They'd moved it a little to the left and a little to the right, and then they created something that nobody else had seen before.

I thought about that for a long time. To me it was such a revelation—it became the basis for the way I think, understanding that there are multiple ways to see something, there are always other perspectives. And just because you don't see what everybody else sees doesn't invalidate your view.

So much of life is just perspective. So change your perspective, look at things differently, and see what else there is to see.

Of course, as a kid you don't really want to see things differently, you don't want to be odd—you want to be like everybody else. You want to blend in. That was true for me like it is for any other young person. Not seeing things the same way other people did, not having the same life experiences as everybody else—it was hard. The house in the desert validated for me that you could be different; that was a big relief. But it still didn't change what was going on in my own home.

CHAPTER TWO

As far back as I can remember, my mother was sick. She was in the hospital anywhere from three to six months out of the year. During those times, my sister Cindy and I only got to see her on weekends when our dad would take us to the hospital in San Francisco. By the time I was five or six I was already thinking about how people carried themselves physically, because I'd learned that there were visiting hours and then there were the times that we were actually able to visit. So if I walked around like I knew what I was doing and looked like I had a purpose, people would just leave me alone. If I walked around looking confused or uncertain, people would bother me.

They'd say, "Hey, what are you doing? Where are you going?" Then they'd tell me, "Visiting hours are over, you can't be here." If I walked around with authority, even though I was a little kid, they'd leave me alone.

Mom was suffering from a whole host of maladies. One of them was kinked intestines. The solution at the time was to go in and surgically remove a chunk of her digestive tract. So she had that done numerous times, I don't even know how many. It was overwhelming as a little guy to get too wrapped up in all the medical issues, but there was no way around it, either.

With my mother being sick all the time, my sister and I were farmed out to different neighbors who would take care of us. Then Dad would come and take us home after work. I can remember being tossed on my father's shoulder with my sister on the other shoulder while he carried us home. That was the greatest. The next morning we would get up and fix our own breakfast. I was in charge of making sure that my sister ate hers. We would have Cheerios, get dressed, and go to school. In the afternoon we would go to whoever's house we were supposed to go to that day.

My mother might have done a lot better if the surgeries had been her only medical issue. But she also had migraines. There was a doctor in Hayward who experimented with electro-shock treatment to try to cure her headaches. And the doctors would give her painkillers—a lot of them. Migraines weren't understood at the time, so to help her deal with the pain they gave her prescription medication. I can only imagine the pain my mother must have been in.

For years she was always trying to find the right dosage or combination of medications to ease the pain. One day in the sixth grade, I came home from school with my father, and she was passed out in the living room on the couch. I could see drool coming out her mouth, and her book was on the floor. My father picked her up under her arms and told me to get her feet. We carried her into the bedroom and put her in bed.

Dad went to the kitchen and got on the phone with the doctor. I still didn't quite understand what was going on, and Dad still hadn't explained anything to me, so I just stood there watching him. After a moment, he put the phone to his chest and told me, "Go on outside, go play. She's breathing. She's okay."

Nobody had to tell me twice to go play. The thing was, even though it was really disturbing to find my mother that way, it wasn't all that much out of the ordinary because there were so many times when my mother was incapable of moving around the house after surgery. We'd bring her meals and go to the library to get her books. If my father was upset, he didn't show it outwardly. I know it threw him for a bit of a loop, but he was very difficult to read. And that was by design. It was common then for men to be that way; that's who he was. I'm very much that way myself.

As more and more time passed, my mom's headaches became more and more frequent. She started trying to figure out what prescriptions she could get from which doctors and how she could get them. That's a whole manipulation of doctors and pharmacists, and it's an incredible feat. I know, because by the time I was ten it was me getting on my bike and going down to the pharmacies for her.

The pharmacists would give me a look and say, "Weren't you here before?" or "I've got to check with the doctor to refill this." There were a lot of questions that started being asked. There were conversations around the house, conversations with different pharmacists, just a whole variety of pieces that I began to put together. It became apparent that she was getting more medication than any of her doctors were aware of. We had three or four different pharmacies that we used.

At the pharmacies, I learned real quick to give non-answers. I understood what my mother was doing because I had seen the pain she was in, so when some pharmacist started to question it, as far as I was concerned I was just protecting somebody I cared about. I wasn't going to throw my own mother under the bus or give her up. You just don't do that.

So I'd tell the pharmacists, "I'm just doing what my mom said" or "My dad told me to come on down." That was as effective a non-answer as I could give. And as a kid I was given a lot of leeway. They'd give me the medication and tell me something like, "Well, the next time you have to have the doctor call it in." But they almost never followed up on that threat. If they did, there was always another doctor.

When Mom was healthy, she was a blast to be around. She was very supportive and intelligent. She'd read a book a day, and we talked about everything—I remember discovering yoga well before it went mainstream in America and having this really fun conversation with her about this totally weird thing people were doing. And Mom was a great cook. She would always have home-made cookies ready for us when we came home from school.

On the weekends she and my father would have their date night. They would drop Cindy and me off with Little Grandma—my father's mother—at her apartment in San Francisco, and we'd fall asleep listening to Billie Holiday, Ella Fitzgerald, and Duke Ellington on her enormous old radio while they went out to the happening jazz clubs.

Mom was the conduit in the family that brought us all together. We'd go camping, or she'd host impromptu barbecues and my dad's apprentices from the elevator repair company would come over with their wives. When everything was going good, it was *on*. But there were many times when it was all off. If Mom got a headache when there had been plans, you had to make excuses.

Spontaneity became important to us if we were going to be able to take advantage of the times when she was feeling good. When she wasn't feeling good, she might be medicated and functioning, medicated and passed out, or medicated and nonfunctioning.

By nonfunctioning I mean she would literally walk into walls. She would take a few steps, stumble, and bang into things. My heart would be breaking and I'd be like, "Mom, just lie down. Let me know what you need." But every person wants to be able to do for themselves. If you're hungry, you want to get up and get some-thing to eat; you don't want to be dependent. There's a real fight psychologically when you say, "If I can take care of myself, I'm not nearly as bad as I think I might be."

So she would get up and try to go into the kitchen, but she couldn't walk down the hall without banging into the walls. If we were reading or watching TV, we could hear her coming, and we would try to either convince her to go back to the bedroom or distract her until she forgot why she'd gotten out of bed, and then we'd bring her whatever she wanted. It was dangerous. If you don't have enough control of your body to be able to navigate a hallway, you certainly don't have the capacity to be around fire or a gas stove. It became a game of manipulation to get her to let us fix her something to eat.

As the pills became a more and more frequent means of my mother dealing with her chronic pain, I would go on over to my friends' houses after school to snack and hang out. I would never invite anyone to my house because I was never certain how my mom was going to be. I didn't want to be embarrassed, or to have her be embarrassed by letting people see her that way.

She was always so frustrated at not being healthy—at not being capable. My father was very frustrated himself because he was try- ing to make money, pay for a house, and provide a decent lifestyle, all on an elevator mechanic's income. I could overhear discussions between my parents and my grandparents about all the medical bills, the insurance, how everything was going to be paid for.

Then Big Grandma, my mother's mother, came and lived with us for a long time. She needed a place to stay, and my parents needed the money for renting her a room, so she moved in and she and my dad would drive up to San Francisco to work every morning. Meanwhile, I would see all these aunts and uncles on my father's side who knew we were under financial stress and wouldn't lift a finger to help. It was never discussed, but even as a kid I resented the hell out of it.

My mother and I had a really strong bond when she was healthy because she did everything she could to make up for the times when she'd slip into her other mode. She taught me to bake frozen cookies for myself after school if she wasn't around to make them from scratch, and to this day I love those. My mom was insistent that I not only learn how to cook, but do laundry and clean house as well. I'd make a bed she could bounce a quarter off. For her, that's just the way it had to be. She was adamant that I would be competent, capable, and independent.

So was I. Only I didn't know what that meant yet, and what it would be good for.

CHAPTER THREE

By the time I was eleven, my treks into the foothills had been getting longer and longer. The hills started two miles from our house and I would go miles beyond that. My parents had no clue as to how far away I went, but I knew it was only a matter of time before they found out. In our neighborhood everybody knew everybody's business, so sooner or later somebody was going to spot me out there and report back to my mom. I didn't care. We had rattlesnakes, mountain lions, and coyotes, and I was a kid on a mission to go out and find them. I'd decided that whatever the consequences, I would have no problem handling them.

Punishment was usually meted out by mom, and it was never a heavy-duty deal. When finally someone told her, "Guess where I saw him," though, she could barely even speak to me except to say, "I'll let your father deal with you."

When I heard my dad come home for dinner I slid a comic book down the back of my pants.

"This is what your son Richard Alan did today," I heard my mother tell him. "I expect you to deal with it."

I was ready. How bad could a spanking really be?

My father opened the door to my room, looked at me, and told me to go into their room. I went in and sat on the bed. He came in behind me and closed the door. My dad was six-one, 215 pounds, big-chested, and he had a belly. He was in his green work garb with his sleeves rolled up over his ropey forearms.

I was totally cool and chilling, looking him in the face. "I know what's happening," I thought. "I got it covered. You can go ahead and smack my bottom because I already figured it out and I got no issues."

My father looked me right in the eyes, full contact, and said, "I'm sorely disappointed in who you are, because you know better. I have higher expectations for you. You gave me less than what was right to give."

Then he turned around and walked out of the room.

The moment, the psychology, it was devastating. It took me a while before I got up and went back to my room.

It hadn't taken my father long to speak his words, but it took me a long time to even begin to understand them—that it wasn't about dealing with punishment, it was about measuring up. It was about making choices and knowing whether or not you were right to do what you'd chosen to do. That was the beginning of going from a kid's perspective to becoming an adult human being.

I hung my head because I had let my dad down. My actions had never been reflected back at me that way before. It was just crushing. I'd thought that I was figuring it all out, living life, having fun—and then to have the tables switched and to be held accountable . . .

You gave me less than what was right to give.

It was just like, "Oh my god! How can you even step into the family after that?" The next morning after a mostly sleepless night, I got up and I had this whole new thing I'd have to figure out. A spanking would have been so much easier.

What I had understood was, *Don't give less than it is right for you to give.*

What I needed to understand next was, *How do you know how much is right?*

I had no idea how much time it would take me before I'd figure out the answer to that question, and that a young kid named Jay Moriarty would be instrumental in it.

* * *

Still, by the summer of '63 I figured I was pretty rocking. I was thirteen, I was training with the Hayward Bluefins Swim Club, and I was getting ready to start my freshman year at Tennyson High, where I'd already signed up for the swim team. Plus, I was making some bank going back and forth between my first two jobs—picking apricots at an orchard nearby and working for a local veterinarian.

Mom and Dad were happy because I was doing what I was supposed to be doing, fulfilling the vision that they had for me that I be productive and involved in my community. Since Mom was in good health, we took the opportunity to make one of our camping trips to Big Basin State Park, about thirty miles outside of Santa Cruz among the redwoods in the mountains overlooking the Pacific. We set up camp at elevation, all warm and toasty in the sun above the notorious Santa Cruz summertime fog. At night we made a fire, cooked out, and slept under the stars. The next morning after breakfast we drove back down through the fog to hit Cowell's Beach back in town.

My mom laid out her towel, wrapped herself up in her sleeping bag, and read her books while us kids dove into the water. I'd been seeing more and more surfers out there lately, and there they were again. By now I was a pretty strong swimmer and had finished junior lifeguard training. Getting knocked around by waves or riding them on my stomach was a lot of fun, but what those older guys were doing on their boards just looked so much better.

They were standing up over the waves, swerving left and right as they glided in toward the beach, and they looked like they were in total control of every motion. I didn't know how they were doing it, but it looked easy. And it looked so *cool*.

After that I started bugging my parents about letting me go surfing. It wasn't that they wouldn't let me, but the cheapest board you could find was about ninety bucks, and I hadn't been working long enough yet to have that much saved up. Then I asked around and found out there was a hotel on the boardwalk that rented surfboards for five dollars a day. That I could afford, so I grabbed my friend Pete and we went surfing the first chance we got.

I liked it right away and even had some success that first day. The paddling out is often the hardest part for a beginner, but since I was a swimmer, I already had some upper body strength and it wasn't any trouble for me. I could stand up on the board, but I couldn't turn because I was way too light to have any real influence on it. Beginner's boards were oversized, nine-plus feet and twenty-two inches wide. At six feet tall and 145 pounds, I didn't have enough weight to actually disrupt the flow of water over the surfboard.

As the whitewater hits the tail of the surfboard, you're supposed to lean toward one rail or the other (the outside edges of the board) depending on which way you want to go. I just sort of stood there with my feet in the right place. Still, there was nothing in the world like being on a wave and just gliding along. These were only knee-high waves, but the sensation of speed and motion was completely exhilarating. Then the wave would just disappear and I'd step off and paddle back out to where I'd started, grinning the whole time.

I don't think I've ever come across anybody who wasn't smiling after they caught their first wave. It's a great way to change your day. *If you're having a bad day, catch a wave.*

It was just so cool, the connection I made with my surroundings. At the same time, I could see guys who were really good, accomplished surfers. They were doing stuff that Pete and I weren't anywhere close to.

I felt I had a pretty good idea of what I was doing, though. It wasn't that complicated. All I had to do was get on the board, point it toward the beach with a little angle on it so it wouldn't go straight in, and, when the whitewater hit, stand up on the board relatively properly and go wherever the water took me. Even with the mistakes I was making, the board was so massive I couldn't mess up the flow. As long as the board was in motion, it pretty much stayed in motion. If you could stand up more or less in the correct place and be semi-athletic, you could get a ride.

We didn't do much of anything except get up and go into what's called the "stink bug stance." That's where your feet are out beyond your shoulder width, your knees are bent, and you're bent at the waist with your arms sticking out from your sides. It's an okay balancing technique. What's better is an athletic crouch, a neutral stance with your feet placed slightly narrower than shoulder-width, but when you first begin surfing your feet go further out than that. That's how you start.

At the time, it was good enough for me, so I saved up for a few months and bought my first surfboard. It was a prefab, low-quality board called a Titan. It had a blue panel board with a clear center and a partial redwood inlay stringer that was only about three-eighths of an inch thick and half an inch wide. The Titan was a pop-out board, which meant it was mass-produced from a mold instead of hand-shaped by a professional surfboard shaper— but for $89 including tax it even came with a car rack. In my opinion, that was a pretty great deal.

The Titan also came with a surf decal, and all the cool cars in the neighborhood were sporting surf decals. My dad had a brand new '63 two-tone, aqua-blue metal flake Chevy Bel Air station wagon at the time—he was not letting that happen.

Armed with my very own gear, it quickly became apparent that I didn't know what I was doing. If all you know is the stink bug stance, your first ride and your first fifty rides will all be the same. Then it isn't so exhilarating anymore. So after my first few surf trips, I started getting frustrated that I couldn't do what the older guys made look so easy. My mind was saying what every kid's mind says when not progressing with something new as fast as they want to: "I'm doing exactly what I see everyone else doing. So why isn't it working for me?"

No one ever told me I was doing the stink bug stance; I thought I was standing there looking exactly like that totally cool guy who was maybe a year or two older than me, standing all confidently with his arms dropped to his sides and starting to stall the board with his shoulders parallel to the nose and tail. He was putting his stall on, bringing up the nose of the board to slow down, and then putting the nose back down and walking the board, trying to get the rail connected with the side of the wave.

It was an advanced move, and I had no idea what I was looking at. Without any background information to process, I had no way to evaluate that we weren't doing the same things at all.

With my lack of progress, my interest in surfing was starting to wane. Surfing seemed fun, sure, but it wasn't the greatest thing since sliced bread. Then I went to the Lane and caught my first overhead—that was the best thing since steamed rice.

One day when I was back at Cowell's Beach (for Santa Cruz surfers, you start your surfing at Cowell's Beach and you finish your surfing career at Cowell's Beach, and who knows where you'll go in between). I figured that rather than catching some waves, I was just going to paddle around.

I decided to paddle all the way up to a spot that I'd heard the older guys call Indicator. I didn't have enough data to know what that referred to; I was just trying to be cool and pick up whatever

I could by listening to the more experienced, confident guys talk. What I picked up was that where the cliff jutted out to cut off Cowell's Beach to the west, that was called Indicator. You couldn't see what was on the other side of the cliff unless you paddled around it. What I learned later was that it was called Indicator because it tells you what's going on at a famous surf spot on the other side of the cliff called Steamer Lane.

So I paddled out past the end of Indicator and looked up toward Steamer Lane. Of course, I didn't know what it was at the time. All I knew was that I could see waves that were way larger than what I'd been riding. I paddled up closer.

There was a little lighthouse up on the cliff, and down in the water I saw these guys catching waves that were over their heads. All the waves I'd ever surfed had been just knee- to waist-high.

These new waves looked like a really awesome time.

I waited until everyone had caught their waves and gone in, then I paddled over for my turn. I saw a wave approaching, turned around and stroked into it. I actually caught it and stood up. Like always, I more or less let the wave take me where it would, but when I started sliding down its face my whole world changed. Making the drop down an eight-foot wave felt like I was flying. It seemed to take forever, and I was going faster than I'd ever gone before. I still wasn't sure what to do, but I was on my feet absolutely speeding through the dark green water, and every cell in my body was screaming, "Oh, *yeah!*"

The drop was so extended that the rush ran straight up through my feet and into my chest as I went. It was so intense, so exciting. And with the speed that it generated, I actually managed to make a bottom turn, then projected out on the shoulder of the wave and made enough of a turn at the top to come back down again.

It was the best. It was what I really wanted.

So I stayed there and kept surfing that spot for a while. When I got back to my buddies at Cowell's they said, "Where did you go?"

I told them, "I don't even know, man."

They didn't know what it was then, either. When I got home that day I was talking to one of the older guys that I knew from swimming and told him where I'd been.

"Oh," he said, "you were at Steamer Lane."

I said, "Wow, man, that was amazing. I caught a bunch of waves there. It was so cool."

With that, my status instantly shot way up. I was no longer just some blond kid hanging out at Cowell's catching small waves. I had actually gone to the Lane and caught overhead waves. I could surf. I could make waves and I could turn. Plus, I got bonus points for doing it on this cheap, little pop-out board. Everything was just wonderful.

What I learned later was that that pop-out board had a fin that was mounted incorrectly and would turn to the right all by itself. So going down the face of the wave and making a bottom turn might have given me this sudden status, and I was thrilled to be able to do it, but really it was just that the fin wasn't mounted straight.

I ended up wrecking my first board the next summer, so I went and got a really good rental board. It was a red, 9′10″ Surfboards Hawaii, in the $125 to $150 price range. I had been picking lots of apricots and was flush with money, and that's what I wanted to do with it. My parents figured it was my money, so I could do what I wanted. The red Surfboards Hawaii was a great board, the proper size for me with the fin mounted correctly, so it helped me learn to surf a lot better.

That first overhead wave, that feeling, that's what got me hooked. That's why I've done what I've done. That's why I ended up surfing Mavericks. And that feeling has never left me.

CHAPTER FOUR

I started going to high school in white dress shirts and ties. That was my grandparents' idea. Cindy and I had been staying with them in August, and they decided to help out my parents by taking us school shopping. Well, I'd never been to high school, so I didn't know. I thought maybe everybody was going to be dressed like me. That wasn't the case at all. The only saving grace was that my mom let me wear my blue Levi's with the shirt and tie. Still, before I ever had a chance to say or do anything, I stood out as odd.

All I wanted was to start practicing with the swim team so I'd look the same as everybody else for a little while, but that didn't pan out either. Just walking into the pool area it was glaringly evident that something was wrong: I didn't even have the proper swimsuit. That's how foreign all of this was. Everybody else was wearing a swimmer's Jantzen or Speedo, and I had on baggies.

That turned out to be the least of my problems.

As a kid you envision yourself in certain situations, doing certain things; being a swimmer was always the vision that I had for myself. It was that basic, that simple—the same as when I surfed for the first time. There was this, *Bam!* I had a vision of being a surfer and being a swimmer. I didn't even know what either really meant, but I knew I wanted to be both.

That's the very first step in anything you want to accomplish: *Have a vision.*

I had a clear picture in my mind of what I wanted to be. It didn't have to be a well-defined picture. That's the great part about being a kid. I started off with something as simple as "I want to be a surfer" and "I want to be a swimmer." However vague, it's how I began the process. And it's something I always remembered when I started to coach people later in life.

The swimming vision went back to when I was that little guy who had no fear of the water. Once I could actually swim, my parents talked around the dinner table about me being on the high school team. But that vision is something that I made my own. I internalized it, aspired to it. *No one can live out someone else's vision; it has to come from within you.* Parents, coaches, peers—you can never reach your full potential if you're tackling a challenge for anyone other than yourself.

So I had my vision. But beginning to fill out that mental picture I'd begun to create was a whole other deal. It was a whole new game.

I'd worked out with the Hayward Bluefins throughout the summer, putting on muscle and getting into decent shape. I'd gotten stronger by placing those demands on my body, but I was only given cursory instruction on how to develop a formal stroke and on the discipline of when and how to breathe. Now I was in the pool with people who were athletes and had all the training. They were blowing right past me.

It sucked. Not knowing where I fit into any of it was truly unsettling. Wasn't I any good? It had never been a question before. Having had some confidence and some ability as a kid swimming around in lakes and the ocean, or just being at free swim in the pool, I was more capable than most of the other kids. But that was nothing like stepping into an organized program where people had received stroke instruction and been doing things long enough to develop efficiency and some strength. They were used to swimming distances. When you're fooling around in the water, you may think you're swimming a long way, but it's not the same.

I was trying to have fun, but it was hard to get beyond the realization that I wasn't measuring up. If I wasn't in the water, I was a pretty shy guy. Now, for the first time in my life, swimming made me uncomfortable as well. I knew I wanted to swim competitively in high school, but I didn't know anything about the work it would take to even begin to achieve it. I didn't even know how to properly take a breath.

I remember watching the other swimmers go by and not even having a clear idea of how to swim lanes—I had to be told. The other kids would bump into me and push me out of the way. And my baggies weren't only a problem because they looked different; they were not conducive to speed, either. They were only good for being discretionary. That first day walking into the locker room and watching everyone, I'd been thinking that when I got into the pool it wouldn't be so strange since nobody would be able to see my trunks. I figured once I was in the water it would all be so much better . . . but then it had gotten so much worse.

As a human being, not even an athlete at that point, all of who I thought I was was suddenly called into question. I'd swim competitively before, but I had never m of how much I did not look like the that surfer stall his board and not real the same things until I'd gotten advanc maneuvers. I had never made the connecti that make up a skill set such as swimming, own individual makeup.

Still, I never thought about dropping it. Now that I could see what the next level was, now that I was aware of what components went into achieving it, I was determined to get there myself. I never said, "I don't want to swim." My personal resolve was to do whatever it took not to be at the bottom.

And to get a pair of Speedos.

My vision of being a good swimmer started to become more defined by being around more experienced, competent athletes. Being a good swimmer now meant swimming not for a minute or a minute and a half, but swimming for twenty minutes and then having a structured workout. You had a certain amount of time to complete a certain distance before you could rest. So if the team had to do 200 yards in four minutes and you could do it in three, you got a minute to rest. The faster you were, the more rest you got. If you were like me in the beginning, you were finishing while the others were starting again. So for me it was constant swimming for the full hour in the beginning.

I would swim until I got cramps in my legs. I would stop because I had never had that kind of pain before. I'd tell the swim coach, "My legs hurt," and he'd just go, "Okay, well you're done for the day." On the way home I could hardly walk. My mom or my dad would rub out my legs and it was so painful I would cry.

At that time taking salt tablets was the solution to cramps. You'd take a handful and that was supposed to fix it. And there were some guys who worked themselves to the point that you'd see them throwing up in the showers after practice. Now I know, f course, that salt tablets and puking aren't good for you. It's an ication that something is out of balance and needs to be recti- Your body cannot be pushed to that level on a daily basis that taking its toll. As a coach I would not encourage that ining, and I would be very concerned if I had an indi- as pushing themselves that hard. Medically, I'd want to know that there wasn't anything wrong. After that, we could be having some very serious discussions about what was going on and at what cost.

When you find yourself going to extremes, a good coach will pull you aside and ask, "What are we really trying to achieve here?"

So I pushed myself to a point just short of throwing up. I would come home and be physically done. Earlier that summer, I had been a kid, running around, surfing, riding bikes, doing all sorts of fun, cool things. Now I would get home and fall asleep. The other kids could do the whole workout like it was nothing. It was unbelievable; I didn't know how I was ever going to fit in with those guys. They weren't exactly making it easy, either.

We had a big meet coming up toward the end of the first quarter and everybody said that they were going to shave their heads or get ridiculously short haircuts. I heard the juniors and seniors talking about how fast they were going to be once they'd shaved down.

Then when I showed up in the lunch room the next day with all my hair chopped off, they all said, "Why did you do that?"

I was like, "Are you kidding? We were *all* going to do this!"

They snickered and laughed at me. I couldn't believe it. It was another embarrassment. It was also a real eye-opener. There are a lot of people who'll talk about what they'll do, they'll tell you any and everything, but most of them don't have any follow through.

But it didn't take very long before I could tell myself, "Wow, this is really cool. I'm progressing." I was starting to be able to keep up with people or stay fairly close instead of being continually lapped. That was a personal achievement, and I acknowledged it. It was just like, "Finally!"

I had the hope and the belief that it would happen, but it wasn't a reality until it actually happened. Once it did, the next step was to be able to start lapping people. It took three months before that started happening. To get there was just so physically and mentally harsh. I mean, I had never been so tired and exhausted.

That first quarter, everything took a backseat to accomplishing that goal.

I flunked every class.

When I was in junior high, I'd gotten all A's. Between swimming and surfing, though, I got real independent about not wanting to study and just blowing off all the scholastics. When I got that first report card, I remember walking home from school thinking about how screwed I was.

"Dad's gonna ground you forever. There's no way to lie your way out of it. This, you're going to have to wear. The consequences are going to be whatever they're going to be, and you're just going to have to deal with it because you created this mess."

I was grounded indefinitely. The worst part, though, was that I had to start going to all of my teachers every week and get a note from them to my parents telling Mom and Dad how I was doing in each class. It was so embarrassing because I had to go set up the whole deal myself, explaining to the teachers that I had not been participating or putting in any effort and now my parents wanted to keep track of what I was doing.

That was all my dad's idea. My mom had nothing to say—I'd screwed up so badly she wouldn't even talk about it.

The next quarter, I started getting A's and B's again.

CHAPTER FIVE

When you start to have success you definitely become more interested in whatever you're doing. I was starting to fulfill my vision, but as a freshman I hadn't made the varsity team and I knew that there were freshmen who had. I wanted to be that good and I didn't like being told that I wasn't, so when swim season started up again in the spring I started increasing my workouts, adding yardage.

The swim coach said that to work on lung development we should be running with the cross country team. That was a real interesting endeavor for swimmers, and most of the guys declined. For me, though, anything I could do to get better I was going to try. Then I found out how good those cross country guys really were. I didn't want to work that hard to be a runner; I'd work that hard to be a swimmer, but not to be a runner.

I was young, numb, and dumb.

By sophomore year, I was definitely over it. I would start the runs with the cross country team, but as soon as we got out of sight I'd find every available pond and go swimming until the runners came back around, then I'd get out and slog along at the end of the pack. When we got back to school I would be as wet as the rest of them.

Still, at that point I was the only swimmer who was doing any running at all, and I'd made varsity.

When I finally won a swim meet in my age bracket it was in a place called Lodi, an agricultural town south of Sacramento about an hour and half from Hayward. They had a real nice training facility. At this particular meet the water was a little cooler than normal, which I liked because I run hot and I perspire very easily. I was swimming the 200-yard individual medley, which finishes with freestyle. I remember out-touching the guy next to me, who I knew from a different team, and I was shocked because that had never happened before.

I had beaten this guy by just half an arm's length. And when I got my time I found out it was a personal best. That was very gratifying because as an athlete you have two elements you have to deal with: *It's always cool to be number one, to win, but if you're not improving on your own performance, winning is negated.*

I'd just beaten somebody, and with that performance, I learned something else about winning that I'd never suspected: *As you become faster than your friends, there begins to be an invisible wall, a little separation.*

I noticed the wall immediately. When I came back to our team prep area, all excited, I learned that I had just bumped somebody else off the best time in our age group for that particular race. The cold shoulder was palpable. Nothing was ever said, but the mannerisms among my teammates had changed. There was a stiff, sullen vibe coming off the guys that hadn't been there before the race.

It was the first time this had happened to me, and at first it was very confusing, but before long I realized, "Oh, *that's* why." A few weeks later the guy I'd bumped posted a better time than me and everything was back the way it had been, no cold shoulder at all. Then I beat him again on my next go-round in that race and it was back to the wall.

It was very subtle. You've entered into someone's personal space, in a way, and it becomes very difficult for the individual to handle the fact that they achieved something that has now fallen by the wayside. But that's the whole deal, you know?

That's all a part of the early stages of becoming an athlete that no one really talks about. How do you deal with it? Well, if you take a look at the bigger picture, there's always somebody better. The first thing that we all have to do is protect ourselves. You've invested and validated who and what you are and what you're working toward achieving, but you have to recognize that in the process there are going to be people you're outpacing and people outpacing you. Each individual has to come up with a way to deal with that.

After my first win, I was very confused for a long time. Since I didn't start doing athletics until I was thirteen, I didn't have any experience or anything to draw on. My coaches and my parents never talked about it. Like a lot of kids, I was left on my own to figure it out.

This is what I realized, eventually: Since there's always somebody better and always somebody coming up, you need to acknowledge each little accomplishment or else you can become overwhelmed by the totality of what you're trying to achieve. But because I knew what my larger goal was, I had a hard time doing that. I'd often fall into the trap of only thinking about the big picture, ignoring the progress I was making along the way.

By discounting my little successes—shaving a second or two off my time, learning to breathe more efficiently, being able to swim a few minutes longer before the pain set in—all I was left with was, "I'm not where I want to be."

That's something every athlete has to be very aware of. A lot of coaches don't let their athletes know it's really important to acknowledge what they have done. Even with the intermediate goals and intermediate achievements, it's very important to receive recognition of the effort you've invested and of your return on that investment. Because by the time you're a senior in high school, that's one of the last periods for a long time that you're going to be top dog in whatever world you're in. Once you step into either college or the workplace, you're up against a lot of other people who are also motivated to achieve and who often have more experience than you. If you go to college, unless you're incredibly fortunate, it takes three or four years until you come back up to the top again. That's a long way to go without acknowledgment.

So you have to break down every goal into smaller, achievable steps, and acknowledge accomplishing each of them.

Everybody has to improve at what they do, whatever they do. Even if you set a world record, it's there to be broken. Your effort was never perfect; it was as perfect as what you could do at the time. That's why you have to learn to review back. You go back to every stroke, every ten yards, whatever it is you can manage, and you start breaking down the race and putting it back together again to recognize what you could have done better. When you're looking at each little aspect and element, it's easier to see how to improve each one of them just a little bit. So the next time you go to do it, it's a new personal record.

But of course I didn't have enough experience to come up with anything like that at the time. I was struggling, and discussing it with friends wasn't going to work—beyond just getting things off your chest, it's not particularly useful to try to figure things out with your peers. At best you're talking to people with just slightly more experience than you have, so there isn't always something there to help a person through.

What I began to understand, and what any athlete has to understand, is this: *You can only compete against yourself.*

My precise thought was, "It's not me beating them, it's me becoming better at what I do. I want to begin to become what *I* can become." That was the beginning of my development of that process.

It was necessary to find that out on my own because there really wasn't much conversation between the coaches and athletes. Coaching was still in its infancy—it was merely the setting of expectations and then, as you became good—well, you were already good, so there wasn't much need to explain anything further. There was very little discussion of technique and stroke and all of that. You just had to get good, and that's all there was to it. And the way you got good was just by getting in and doing more laps.

The vast majority of kids receive completely inept coaching, not because the coaches don't care, but because they just don't understand. Most of them are volunteers and they only do it because they care about the kids. The problem is they don't have much personal understanding of how to communicate well or any clue about setting goals and building skill sets.

When you're exposed to a really sophisticated sports program where they talk and think and create understanding in both their coaching staff and in their athletes, you see there's a very definite drop-off in coaching quality in the lesser programs, because it takes time for all of that sophistication to be validated and then to filter down through the cracks. And by the time it reaches young kids, kids who are, in my opinion, way too young to be involved in sports—three and four years old—you're getting coaches who just default back to what we had in the early sixties, which wasn't working then either. You know, "Just go do more laps."

George Haines was different.

CHAPTER SIX

George Haines was the coach of the Santa Clara Swim Club. That was the elite swim team in Northern California, and Haines was the elite coach. At Tennyson High, we were issued sweat suits so that when we went to meets we would look like a team. Then we saw the suits that the Santa Clara club was wearing, and they were a whole different generation—they looked like something the Olympic team might wear.

In fact, during the 1964 Summer Olympics, we'd see some of Haines' swimmers competing on TV, and then we'd go to meets and see them doing warmups in the same pools we were using. It was fascinating; they weren't even adults yet, but some of them were already world-class athletes.

They included swimmers like Don Schollander and Donna de Varona. We'd see them on *Wide World of Sports,* but when they were at the pool they just looked like normal kids, even when they were signing autographs. Well, they *looked* normal, but they didn't *swim* normal. They were more than just a lot faster. In equal competition by age and grade, they just left the whole pool behind. They were that good. Then we could go into the dressing room and hear them talking and, again, they were just like normal kids.

We all wanted to be that good.

As early as sophomore year I was going to meets at the swim center in Santa Clara every chance I got to watch how Haines' team worked out and hear what he said to his swimmers.

He talked stroke. He broke things down into what today we call skill sets—the angle your arms should be at and things like that. Of course, anything George Haines said were words from God. And his swimmers did all these exercises none of us had ever even heard of. For instance, he had some of his guys swimming laps in their sweat suits. I thought it was the weirdest thing I'd ever seen, but if they were doing it, I was going to do it.

I think I made it through two practices in my sweats before my own coach called it off. "That's enough," he told me. "Get them off."

"But the Santa Clara team was doing it," I said. "I saw them!"

He just said, "Yeah, well, you've got a ways to go yet."

Another thing I saw Haines' swimmers doing was to attach a rope to a bucket and then swim pulling the bucket after them. It was simple resistance training, but at the time I had no idea about that. But, again, if that's what they were doing, and they were better than me, then I had to do it to be that good. That was the logic. My coach still didn't share my enthusiasm. He explained that I had to have better form before I started working on developing that kind of strength.

On that point I have no doubt he knew what he was talking about, but I was in a real rush to get as good I could be as fast as I could. What we had discussed in the family was that if I became a good enough swimmer I could get a scholarship to college. Since my parents didn't have any money to speak of, that was really my only shot at getting an education.

Swimming was also providing something crucial that I had trouble finding anywhere outside of the sport—girls.

The Bluefins club was a mix of boys and girls. Initially, I was much too shy to talk to the girls but as I got older, maybe sixteen or so, I started to get over it. It was great just being able to hang out in a familiar environment while I was learning to be around these strange creatures. Just getting to talk to them was amazing. It was a really nice casual setting for me to start to open that door.

For me, girls were just—well, they weren't boys. They were so different . . . unless they were swim girls. The girls who swam—it was much easier to have conversations with them. We were all talking about the same types of things. Other girls were either very academic, and all they wanted to talk about was school, which wasn't interesting to me. With swim girls, though, we could talk about the meets coming up, how we were going to get there, what events we were in.

I was never the standout swimmer in any one discipline, but I could swim lots of things pretty well. I might not be number one or two in an event, but I might be a great number three in several, and when you're trying to win at swim meets, you pick up points for the number of people on your team that place. So they would put me in a lot of events to gain more points that way. Instead of just swimming freestyle, I'd swim freestyle plus backstroke and breaststroke at various distances. Girls from the swim teams actually understood all that because they dealt with it themselves. Despite my shyness, it began to feel natural to be around them in the pool at practices.

It was around this time that my mom said, "I think we need to get you a jockstrap."

"Mom, what're you talking about?"

"Well, your Speedos are little too revealing and maybe we should get—"

"Mom!" I yelled. "You're not supposed to look!"

I decided to wear two suits for a while.

By junior year I was a lot more socially adept. I was starting to date, and I was having a lot more success at surfing and swimming. There was plenty of time for all that fun stuff because a lot of us older guys on the team had figured out that you only needed to maintain a C average to get a swimming scholarship, so I had started to slack off in my classes again.

That didn't fit with my parents' vision, of course, but I was growing more and more independent. And that was part of their vision, too, wasn't it?

Toward the end of the school year, my mother asked me, "Who are you thinking of taking to the Junior Prom?"

I said, "Huh? Mom, I'm not going to the Junior Prom."

"Richard Alan, of course you're going to the Junior Prom. That's what boys do."

"Mom," I told her, "I only have so much money. It costs $150 to get a new surfboard, and if I go to the prom I'd have to spend it all on that. Summer's coming up and you don't use the same boards in the summer that you use in the wintertime and they want that money up front. I will have way more good times with a new board than I would taking a girl to the prom."

My mom told me, "This is something you'll regret. How can you forgo this experience? The surfing thing is going to go by the wayside and you're going to look back and regret this."

"I'm not going to put my money there," I said. "It ain't happening."

She had wanted me to do the whole deal of bringing the girl on over to meet her and see me all dressed up, pinning the corsage, all the stuff that she had pictured for that particular moment. I wasn't coming through for her.

It's just that I knew what my priorities were and where I would draw the line. Taking a girl to the prom might have provided some of the lifelong memories my mother was talking about. Then again, it might not have. Surfing, though, that *was* life. It was the deep end of the pool. I wanted to go *there*.

So I went there, all summer long, and when I came back to school as a senior my slacking reached world-class levels. My buddy Pat and I were skipping out all the time to go surfing. We didn't know anything about surf forecasting, but there was a network of surfers and we always let each other know when the surf was good.

When it was, I'd say, "Hey, Pat, why don't you go by my house and pick up my board?"

And I would go by his house to get his board. So if either of us ran into the other guy's mother we could just say, "Oh yeah, he told me I could use his board."

For us, we knew which teachers we could slide on and which would give us grief. As far as college went, I didn't even have to fill out any applications because there were schools that were interested in me. One was Southern Oregon College, but they couldn't offer anything in terms of a scholarship. The guy's pitch was that it was this great little community at the base of a mountain where I could learn to go skiing and do a lot of other outdoor activities—but they didn't include surfing. So it was enticing, but not enough to get excited about.

Meanwhile, the University of South Carolina at Hancock sent me a package for a full-ride swimming scholarship. All I knew about South Carolina was that it's on the ocean—it had surf. I could do all the college stuff I wanted to do, plus I could catch waves. It was fine by me to go to the east coast because being in California I had no clue how fortunate I was, surf-wise. So here was a school offering a full scholarship and it was close to the beach. I had a very serious interest in it and I was trying to envision myself being there.

My mom told me straight out, "That's not going to work."

"But Mom," I said, "this is like totally cool."

"It's not going to work."

"But why?"

"Because I know you, Richard Alan, and I know how you were raised. You're going to have issues."

Well, in 1967 there were a lot of race-related incidents being reported in the news. In Hayward there were a lot of white, Portuguese, and Hispanic families and a few Asian families. Then at the beginning of my senior year, the first black family moved in. As was the custom with our family, when somebody new moved into the neighborhood, you went on over with a homemade loaf of bread or some cookies and welcomed them. So that's what I did.

There was a guy about my age, Walt, his younger sister, and their mom and dad.

On the first day of school I borrowed the family car and drove Walt and some other kids over with me. We rolled in and I was oblivious to anything. I just didn't see the issue. It turned out that some people thought the NAACP had moved Walt's family in to start making inroads into Hayward. That whole controversy flew right over my head because in my life judgment had always been based on somebody's value. To me, it had always been: *Either you bring something to the table and you're cool or you don't bring anything to the table, in which case why would I hang out with you?*

You meet people and it doesn't take very long to figure out whether they're interesting and can carry on a conversation or if there's just nothing there, no synapses firing. It's got nothing to do with race or gender or class.

So when I watched the news and saw all the racial tension, especially in the South, I just didn't make the connection. I thought, "That's someplace else. We're here. This is our neighborhood."

My mom was flipping out about me going to South Carolina. She was afraid that I wouldn't be able to grasp that there was a race conflict going on. How could you expect people to go to the back of the bus? How could you divide a diner? My mom knew it would make no sense to me, that I would walk into any restaurant and speak to anyone.

Once I understood my mother's concern, it still didn't make me give up on going to South Carolina. It was a real opportunity, I was old enough to make my own decisions, and it required a lot of consideration.

Then late in the school year my father had a stroke and couldn't work anymore. Suddenly, college was no longer on the table.

PART II
YOUNG, NUMB, AND DUMB

CHAPTER SEVEN

When I was about eight, my father and I were walking to his work truck from our house when a car drove by and the driver waved at him. My dad waved back.

I'd never seen the car or the driver before, so I asked, "Oh, who's that, Dad?"

"I have no idea," he told me.

"Then why did you wave?"

His response was, "If somebody takes the time to wave to me, I should take the time to wave to them."

* * *

In life, none of us ever signs up for what we get, which is probably just as well because otherwise we might choose not to live at all since so much of life can be disappointing. My dad is a case in point. He was the youngest of four and living in San Francisco with his family when his father went out to get a loaf of bread and never came back. I have no idea how the family survived after that. It was never spoken of. All I know is that it was not good. When my dad met my mom in the early 1940s, he didn't have a job, so his oldest sister's husband got him one delivering towels.

Somewhere along the way he became an elevator mechanic; my uncle did the towel deliveries his entire life.

Before my mom got sick they used to go hunting and camping and hang out with the people that my mom grew up with on the western edge of the foothills of the Sierras. They would do cattle drives and my dad would ride bulls. He was quite a character, and they always told Cindy and me about all the great times they'd had.

To have me, my mom went through thirteen or fourteen miscarriages, so it was a miracle that I was even born. I was the survivor of twins.

I think my dad was very frustrated. He was looking at me and my sister thinking, "Here are these kids that are supposed to go to college." He had been telling us ever since we were little that that's what was going to happen. But with my mom's illnesses and the constant medical bills, he couldn't afford it.

He worked constantly. When he broke some ribs, he just taped them up and went back to work. He broke fingers, too, and I can remember several stories about him being electrocuted to the point of incapacitation, but he always got up and went back to work the next day. That was it—that's what you did. I really can't imagine facing all of that, even though in my own life I've faced a lot of struggles.

Going to the bar was my dad's break.

People at the bar called him Big Lucky. He played dice and had a reputation around town. Every once in a while I would sneak into the bar and overhear him. Dad never really displayed any emotion—which, again, was a typical male thing—but when he was gambling you could hear it. Another side of him emerged when he was shooting dice with his pals. Big Lucky was boisterous, engaging, and fearless.

I remember he made an attempt at getting our family to socialize with some of the families of the other guys from the bar. The bars around town had their own baseball teams and they'd set up camping trips and things like that, so my dad figured he'd get us involved. My mom was not keen on it at all. It didn't work out. There were arguments at home about "those people."

South Hayward wasn't the best of neighborhoods. It wasn't the worst, but it had its problems. There were several stories of people coming in to rob the bar and my dad telling them, "This is my bar and if you want to rob it you're gonna have to go through me. So figure out what you want to do."

This guy who had already robbed the bar once came back with a gun while my dad was in the bathroom. When my dad came out he assessed what was going on, broke a beer bottle on the way to the front door and just said, "You're leaving here or you're going through me." Luckily, the guy managed to get out the back exit.

We wouldn't hear these stories from my father, of course. These are stories that would reach us through other people. They would horrify my mother, but as a kid I would tell myself, "That's *my* dad!"

There was a flip side to his reputation that I wasn't so proud of. With everybody knowing everybody's business in our neighborhood, I'd often overhear people talking about my parents. You know, "Oh, that's that kid whose dad goes to the bar every night and his mom is sick."

To have it be known and disapproved of hammered home the message that we were not a normal family. It was difficult knowing that everybody knew. It was embarrassing if for no other reason than the fact that none of the kids I knew had dads who hung around bars and mothers who were sick. Obviously, many other people had similar issues, but growing up I didn't understand this. As far as I knew, nobody else in our little development was dealing with anything like our family did.

As kids we got around the neighborhood by walking fences. They were six feet tall with four-inch-wide two-by-fours along the tops, and, once you got good at balancing on them, you could practically run on them around all the houses and through every yard in the development. Early one Saturday morning I was fence-walking to my friend's house when I heard a couple talking as I walked past their yard. They were talking about my father.

They were saying that he was a drunkard, just hanging out at the bar all the time. It made my face burn. It hurt.

Even though my dad had a drinking issue, he never showed how much he drank. From the time I was twelve, though, my mom would say, "Would you call the bar and find out if your dad's there? It would be nice of him to come home. You know, I've got dinner waiting." At sixteen, when I started to drive, she would ask me to go by the bar to see if he was there.

He was a big, tall man who was quite capable of moving around with confidence, so it was never really discernible that he had been drinking. He would come home from the bar, have dinner with us, then sit back in the La-Z-Boy and in ten minutes he'd be asleep, snoring with his eyes open. We never really knew if he was drunk; although we could smell the alcohol, he was always up the next morning like he had never had a drop.

In fact, it was my dad who woke me up at five every morning so I could get in a workout before school. I'd fix us breakfast and we'd have talks just between the two of us. He was a morning person, always real social and happy at the start of the day.

Then he came home one night and started bouncing off the walls in the hallway just like my mother did when she was medicated. It was the first time in my life that I'd ever seen him unable to walk a straight line. No matter what amount of alcohol my father consumed, he always had a steady gait and he could always carry on a conversation. He had clear, bright eyes, so you could never tell if he'd had one or a whole bunch. But now he was stumbling into walls.

My mom was very upset. We were all in shock because it was so frightening to see him being anything other than competent and capable.

"Something is wrong with him," my mother said. "I need to take him to the hospital."

When she got there, the doctor told her, "He's just drunk. Get him out of here. There's no reason for him to be here, so stop wasting our time."

The next morning Dad hadn't improved at all. He was slurring his words and one side of his face was all slack; the muscles didn't function. Mom took him back to the hospital, and she came home alone that time because he'd been admitted as a stroke patient. She was livid because the doctors had blown it so badly that he could have died.

We were lucky he hadn't died, but he was incapacitated by the stroke and lost the use of one side of his body. Just like that, everything changed for us as a family. We had to sell the house and move into an apartment. We'd never lived in an apartment before. Moving out of the house we'd lived in for fourteen years, getting rid of all the things we'd accumulated—it didn't take more than that to tell us that nothing would ever be the same again.

We packed everything up and moved a mile down the street into an apartment building. It was way too small. I was used to having a garage to work out in, and now all we had was a tiny patio off the living room and a minute kitchen. With the neighbors all around us, we could smell their cooking in the hallways and hear their arguments through the walls.

I'd saved up $400 washing dishes at Perry's Boy Smorgasbord that winter to buy a beautiful, deep green '52 Chevy Deluxe wagon with imitation wood side panels; now I had to leave it parked in the street and start riding my bike again because I couldn't afford the auto insurance. I would chain the bike to the handrail on the stairway, look longingly at my station wagon, and go upstairs.

Obviously, it was Dad who suffered the worst of it. Beyond the physical devastation, there was a mental and emotional hell that he went through. Here was a man who went to work every day. It didn't matter what else happened, it was expected that you went to work. You could have double pneumonia—you went to work, that was the deal. Now my dad was home all the time in that little apartment. He couldn't even dress himself.

Of course he never talked about it, but you could tell he wasn't a happy boy. There wasn't any swagger left in him, and he would kind of slump in his chair looking suddenly old and small. His whole world had been reduced to that little apartment—there was no more bar, no more beer or cigarettes, no more Big Lucky.

My mom meanwhile went from the one being taken care of to being the caretaker. I didn't know what we were going to do if she got sick or had an episode before my father got well again. If he ever did get well again.

He did begin to slowly recover, though, and my dad would rally his spirit from time to time. When he did, we got to see a more charming side of him. He would crack jokes and give a half-smile with a sparkle in his eye, but he never did go back to work again.

For me, college was definitely on hold, maybe even cancelled altogether. We went on welfare and food stamps. Nobody could afford anything. We had no money, so there were greater concerns than school. For instance, how were we going to make it as a family?

CHAPTER EIGHT

It was expected that I would work because I was capable of working and contributing to the well-being of the family. While there was definitely a downside to living in a community where everybody knew what was going on with everybody else, the upside was that there was a strong sense of, well, community. Since everybody knew that we needed money, it was arranged for me to start coaching the little kids in the Bluefins swim club.

I never even knew how much I was being paid—the money went straight to my parents.

As a senior, before my dad's stroke, I'd been discussing my plans for the future with my coach, Tom Crocker, who'd been running the Bluefins as well as the high school team since the summer before my junior year. He would drive me to swim meets and we got a friendship going. He knew that I had wanted to study coaching and art in college, so all the pieces were already in place for him to offer me the job. It was an easy transition since I was already on the team and both the kids and the parents knew me.

It worked out great because it meant I didn't have to take the time to find a job on my own and it allowed me to keep doing everything I needed to do as far as swimming and surfing were concerned just by giving up a little bit of free time. To this day,

I have no idea what the compensation was—the money I was making went straight to my parents—but I just figured, *When you don't have anything at all, every little bit goes a long way.*

The assignment I was given was to coach the ages six to ten. I was stoked because I would be supervising what their workouts were going to be and discussing with Tom what he was looking to achieve for their age groups. I thought that they were all cool, and they thought I was the cat's meow because I was older.

We had a really nice thing going, but there was not a whole lot that I knew at the time to be able to work with them. For the most part I would just end up babysitting them when they were swimming. Even though I had some background, I still wasn't comfortable enough to be able to talk to them about stroke technique—I didn't understand it enough myself. I had been exposed to it by watching George Haines and his coaches discuss it with their swimmers, but it wasn't something that was talked about on our team. I was just watching the kids do laps and keeping track of the clock.

Whatever I was being paid, it wasn't much. Anything we wanted to do had to go through a process of "Can we afford it?" Even though my family had never had a lot of money, we were always able to go camping or go out to dinner, all sorts of little things. Now even those little things were out of the question.

We ate a lot more soups, and while we used to have chuck roast or London broil now and then, now we went to all-hamburger when we had any meat at all. My mother was making Hamburger Helper before Hamburger Helper was invented to make the meat go further by adding macaroni or rice.

As a growing young man and an athlete, I had to eat, and I figured that since we were buying cheaper food, at least I could eat as much as I wanted of it. Then one night my father was at the table, my mother was over by the stove, and I went for my third helping of dinner.

"Richard," my mother said, "you can't eat that much anymore."

That was so major. It must have been very hard for my mother to have to tell me that. My father had tears in his eyes. He didn't say a word.

When my father had recovered enough to be able to get around on his own, he won a five-minute shopping spree that a new supermarket had given away as a grand opening promotion. Even though he still had trouble walking and using one of his arms, he was on a mission. He pre-thought it, analyzed it, and knew exactly where he was going so that there was no time wasted. Hitting the big ticket items first, Dad filled a whole shopping cart with meat before he went back in for the pasta and rice. We didn't have a proper freezer in the new place so we had to store most of it with friends, but we still ate pretty well for a while.

My father had always really enjoyed food shopping. Prior to the stroke he would take the family to a supermarket called Big Top every Saturday. He knew everybody—the butchers, the green grocers, the fruit sellers. He would laugh and chat with them and they always had special stuff set aside for him. They would tell him what was coming in during the week, and, if he wanted something, they would hold it back for him. But that market was more expensive, so when we went on food stamps the Saturday shopping trips stopped.

Dad started doing the shopping at a cheaper market by himself during the week. I think he didn't want us to see him using food stamps. Besides, once he had to change stores, the experience was no longer the same. The friendly exchange that went on between the grocers and a regular customer was gone. Instead of selecting specific, fresh cuts of meat from the butcher with whom he'd had a relationship, now everything was prepackaged.

There are a lot of subtle little things that change when you no longer have bank. You're still shopping, you're still getting food . . . but it's all different.

*   *   *

After graduation, I continued to coach the kids into the summer, and I also got a job as an usher at a new movie theater that had opened in town. I had to wear a hideous orange jacket and black slacks, but it was great for being able to see movies for free. More importantly, I got to see all of my friends, and they'd let me know what was happening with the surf.

By working two jobs I was able to help my family out and start paying the insurance on my Chevy again, and the guys at the theater always knew if I'd been surfing because I kept my board strapped to the roof at all times. It was summer and, as a surfer, you always want to be ready to catch one more wave.

A group of lifeguards came into the movie theater one night. We all knew each other from the swimming circuit. This guy Doug Pearson was the head lifeguard at a lake called Cull Canyon in the East Bay area.

We got to talking and Doug told me, "Hey, you should come be a lifeguard with us. Come on by tomorrow and we'll get you taken care of."

So I went on over the next day and a whole crew of characters that I knew were working there. There was Doug's brother, Bob, Mike Lapin, Jim Locke, and a few other guys from the circuit. They were all heading to either Chabot Junior College or Cal State Hayward in the fall. I had the same swimming skills as them and I picked up CPR training and got my lifeguard certification through that group.

Once I started lifeguarding at Cull Canyon, I had to quit coaching the Bluefins. I appreciated the effort from the community and from Tom Crocker, but it just wasn't very challenging, I wasn't learning anything so phenomenal that it was worth the investment of time. Plus, I'd just graduated high school and I wanted to be around people my own age a lot more.

The second hardest part about being a lifeguard, I learned, is getting accustomed to doing visual sweeps and staying focused while you're in the chair, and communicating with the guys working with you on the ground so you can respond immediately and appropriately to any situation that arises. The vast majority of the time there's nothing going on, but you develop an intuitive sense when watching people's movements to the point that you can pick up on it when something isn't right. If one or more people look like they're having trouble, you could casually send someone over to check on them so that you wouldn't have to shut down the lake. If you had to grab the paddleboard to go make a rescue, the lake would shut down and all the guards would start blowing whistles and pulling everybody out of the water.

The swimming lake was in the rolling hills above a retention lake that was used as an emergency reservoir. There was fishing in the lower lake, and people would invariably fall into it because the sides were steep and folks had a habit of drinking. Some of those rescues were successful, some were not. When you can't rescue someone—that's the hardest part about being a lifeguard.

My first experience with death, though, was when some kids came running over and said that one of the adults was passed out in his car in the parking lot. I ran out and opened the car door. I could see that the man was dead, but as a lifesaver I didn't have the authority to designate whether someone was living or dead. My obligation was to do everything in my ability to make sure he had oxygen and try to revive him, so I gave the man mouth to mouth. He was clammy and cold and obviously dead, but I kept administering CPR until the fire department showed up a few minutes later and took over.

One of the firemen told me later, "You did everything you could do. He was probably dead before you got here. But we can't pronounce him dead. We're taking him down to the hospital. The physician on duty will make the determination. But," the fireman added, "he's dead."

I went home and couldn't get the dead man out of my head. There really was nothing I could have done. That was upsetting, but it was also a relief. If there had been another option that, through negligence or a lack of training, I had failed to try, I would have had to live with that on my conscience. *I reviewed the experience over and over and over again to make sure I did everything that was within my experience and training.*

A week later I got two letters. One said that the man didn't have any diseases I would need to be concerned about. The other was a commendation from the fire department saying job well done. I had never thought about whether the guy had had bronchitis or pneumonia or tuberculosis. That wasn't part of the training.

*   *   *

When you're working with people, and other people's lives depend on your successful communication and participation, you end up developing a bond. Some of the guys couldn't handle the responsibility of being a lifeguard, and they didn't last long at the lake. But the rest of us who stayed on grew real close.

At one point, some friends of Doug and Bob Pearson's parents rented us a house about fifteen minutes from Santa Cruz for $50 a month. Ten of us went in together at five dollars each. It was great.

Bob and I started hanging out a lot and driving down together in his VW Bug—gas was like nineteen cents a gallon then. He was good at fixing spaghetti dinners and I'd make oatmeal with raisins for breakfast. We'd go to the beach from the cabin, surf, and leave just in time to get to work. If the surf was good, after work we'd head right back to the cabin.

Bob and I both had developed an interest in shaping surfboards. Since we used paddleboards at Cull Canyon and Doug was the head lifeguard, he talked upper management into letting us each design one by telling them we could do it more cheaply than their regular supplier. So we were given a budget, we bought our blanks, and we started a debate about which board designs would work best that still rages to this day.

Bob was always outgoing while I was the loner of the group, but we shared a philosophy of being very inclusive. If we were having a party at the cabin, we wanted everyone to come. We wanted everyone to come and play and participate and have a really great time. If there was anything we could do to help someone have a good time, it was done. If someone liked watermelon, we'd make sure there were watermelons there.

It was such a bummer that summer was drawing to a close and Bob and everyone else in the crew were going to start college without me.

Well, that's what *I* thought.

CHAPTER NINE

I couldn't go away to school, but my parents were still adamant that I go to college. After the drama of my father's stroke, I had thought that that was out of the window, but my parents made it known in no uncertain terms that with summer vacation being over, splitting my days between some dead end job and riding waves was not going to happen. The problem was that I hadn't filled out any college applications, which meant that going to the state university in Hayward wasn't going to be an option. One thing I'd learned in high school, though, was that if I had a problem I should go find a coach. So on the first day of the fall semester I showed up at Chabot, the local community college, and found the swim coach in his office.

"I'm Richard Hesson," I said. "I went to Tennyson High."

"I'm Bob Brown," the coach said. "And I know who you are."

"Things changed in my life. I want to attend Chabot."

"I can take care of that," he said. "But one thing you should know is that all of my swimmers are water polo players."

"Well, I've never played water polo before. I don't even really know what that is."

"It's just a different kind of workout than what you're used to," he assured me. "Meet me back here at the office tomorrow." Then he handed me a schedule and told me, "These are the classes you will attend."

It was that simple.

During the first two weeks of water polo practice, Coach Brown took me aside and said, "I need a goalie."

Because all I had ever done was swim, and because I hadn't played any ball games since junior high, I was great at the swimming part of the game but inept at throwing and catching, so I didn't know why Coach Brown was coming to me.

"I'm talking to you," he explained, "because you have a big voice and I need someone who can command the pool. I have a goalie, but he's graduating in the spring. I want you to take the attitude that this is your pool, that you own it. And I need you to communicate to the team what's going on and what you want them to do."

I was like, "It's *my* pool?"

"Yep."

"This is totally awesome."

I grew into my role rather quickly. Owning the pool was such a complete conceptual change for me. I had been raised in public pools. A pool was a pool and everyone had a right to be there. Someone else cared for them and monitored what was happening—it wasn't on me. Now it was my responsibilty to care for and monitor what was going on and how everyone behaved in the pool—my pool. That meant that if I didn't like what someone was doing, it was, "Not in my house."

The goalie who was ahead of me ended up stepping aside halfway through the first season and just going, "Rock on, kid."

I had a great time. I'd never been given that much responsibility before, and I took it very seriously. Despite having that responsibility along with the confidence in my ability to pull it off, it still didn't register with me that attending class was a particularly important part of the college experience.

The professors had been very clear from the start about what I needed to do to succeed. They told me that the midterm and the final would determine my overall grade for the semester. All I wanted to do was surf, and because I read a lot, I had figured out in high school that I didn't necessarily have to pay attention to what was going on in class. I just had to past tests. So I decided that I didn't need to attend class if I could read all the course materials on my own. Instead, I'd go into the dining center early in the morning and find out who was heading to the beach. The surfers would always meet up there to take a look at one another's schedules and see who was free to catch waves.

At the end of water polo season and the first quarter, Coach Brown found out that I hadn't been attending classes. I had been very successful on my midterms and finals, so I figured I was good, but Coach Brown had gone to all my professors and said, "I need this kid in class. He can't pass."

With him stepping in, I got a withdrawal or a failure in almost every one of my courses. I was so screwed—again.

What the coach told me when I went to see him in his office was, "I know who you are, and you are way too smart to have this much freedom and not have someone to hold you accountable."

It was just like the lecture my dad had given me years before: *You are accountable for your actions. Don't give less than what is right for you to give.*

Except this time I didn't see that I'd done anything wrong. Young, numb and dumb all over again.

Coach Brown explained, "There is so much that goes on in the classroom that you need to experience and pick up. College is about so much more than just a midterm and a final."

All I came back with was, "That's not fair, man. I passed those classes."

He just shook his head at me. "No, you didn't."

I knew how well I'd done on those tests, but it didn't matter. My official grades were withdrawals and failures. To be able to participate in swimming and water polo when the season started up again in the third quarter, I would need a 2.0 with no failures.

"Well, that really sucks," I complained. "This is so unfair."

Leaning forward across the desk, Coach Brown told me, "This is not about being fair. I know too much about you already and I know that what you're doing is not going to benefit you in the long run. I need you in class."

It set a tone for me for understanding that there really is a lot more to learning than passing tests. Nowadays, when I teach a course in construction, so much of the knowledge, experience, and expertise that gets passed along is just through the conversations in the classroom. It gives value to the relationship between the instructor and the students, as well as between the students themselves. Merely passing the tests didn't help me gain the personal experience of class interaction.

But back then I was very rebellious and I just did not want to get in line. Class moved very slowly, and it was frustrating because I really believed I could get what I needed just by reading the material. I could read quickly and form my own opinions. To be in class and to be asked to discuss the reading felt like a waste of time because *I* already knew what I thought of it.

What did fascinate me about college was being on campus watching people as they engaged with one another. There were the kinds of people who would feel compelled to obey Visiting Hours if someone they loved got sick, and people who would come and go as they pleased. Usually in the Athletics Department the vast majority of people moved with some sense of confidence and capability and carried themselves with more focus. Then, when

I watched the general population on campus, there were a lot more people who weren't comfortable or focused.

I thought, I don't ever want to be those people. *I want to be a person who's very comfortable and confident all the time.*

That aspect of my personality really came to the forefront with water polo. Before that I was just a normal guy, not exactly brimming over with confidence. True, I had thought about body movement at the hospital when I was a kid; I had felt how the other guys on the swim team had stiffened up when I won my first meet; I had been watching my mom and dad lose physical control—and I was constantly trying to achieve control of the surfboard—but it was only that first year in college that I really started putting it all together.

When Coach Brown had said, "I want you to understand that this is your pool," it set off a chain reaction. It was a process that took months to get there—it didn't happen overnight—but it happened. I interpreted it as having a responsibility to all of the other players to be able to do a really good job at something. As a swimmer, almost everything you do is for yourself and by yourself. Having a responsibility to other people got me very excited.

What happens in water polo is that there's a player called the hole man who stays in front of the other team's goalie. The idea is that you can make a pass to the hole man, but someone from the goalie's team should be blocking him from catching the pass. Otherwise, the only person in the hole man's way is the goalie, and there's a lot of things the hole man can do to score when left unattended. But for some reason, the hole man was pretty much considered sacrosanct. Nobody would bother him. For me, it was like, "Why would I want to leave that guy unattended and unbothered?"

I hardly knew anything yet but I wasn't letting anybody in my pool go ahead and be there without consequence. Someone was going to dictate to me in *my* pool? I didn't think so.

The whole thing about water polo is that you don't really know the game until you can get below the surface of the water; you have to see what goes on down there. That's where you see all the banging, the hitting each other with elbows and knees; that's where the true aggression of the sport comes out. It's a brutal game.

There are a lot of rules and the refs are watching, but, as soon the game starts and the water is churning, it's impossible to see everything that's going on. We learned real fast that opposing players had no issue with snapping the cord in your swimsuit to make you stop for an instant and miss an opportunity to score. That was polite compared to what else they'd do.

One of the first tournaments we went to, we were watching two top teams play, and the nature of the sport emerged before our eyes. When someone is interfering with your elbows, it becomes very difficult to make accurate passes, and we could see that was happening to the guy who had the ball. Then, seemingly out of nowhere, the opposing player who'd been trying to block the forward flinched, held his face and called Time Out.

Well, that was really bizarre because a player never calls Time Out—only a coach is supposed to do that. The player swam to the edge of the pool and the coach didn't know what was going on when he got up to meet him. Then the player took his hands away from his mouth and handed something to his coach.

It took us a second to realize what it was: his teeth.

"That's it," the coach said. "You're coming out of the game."

The guy told him, "Not a chance," and swam back in. When the game resumed, it wasn't five minutes before the guy who had initiated the tooth loss called Time Out and swam over to hand some teeth over to his own coach to hold onto for later.

I was stunned by the whole display, totally in shock. I also understood the first guy who got his teeth knocked out wanting to get back into the game. The rules had now been clarified: "If this is how you want to play, Game On."

It's not how I wanted to play, though. I was a physical person, but not a violent one. And I especially hated the idea of emotions running so completely unchecked. The lack of control, the utter absence of personal discipline—it was the antithesis of everything I liked about athletics. I was a mischief maker, not a troublemaker. I'd do what I had to in order to succeed, but not if that meant resorting to physical violence.

The problem was that I knew the opposing team's hole man would want to beat the shit out of me. I wasn't going to let that happen.

So I started to harass the hole man endlessly. Being a good swimmer, if someone threw the hole man a bad pass I would come out of the goal and go for it. The hole guy was usually someone who weighed well over 200 pounds because you wanted somebody in there with enough physical mass that he wouldn't be distracted by somebody banging or hanging on him. I was a big boy, usually close in size to the hole man, and usually a faster swimmer. Since the hole man was slower than I was, he wasn't as willing to make moves. I could anticipate the flight of the ball, and I was more than willing to come out and take possession.

As the team learned one another's moves, my teammates knew that if I came out of the goal and went after the ball, it meant I was in my aggressive mode and they had to get somebody up for me to pass to—Bob Pearson was on the team, and he became one of my key guys to throw to. We would set up plays off of that and we became pretty good pretty quick.

Before long I figured out that if I could become annoying enough, I could take the hole man's focus off of scoring and turn it toward getting even with me. The hole guys were used to dominating and intimidating, so it was easy to get them distracted enough that they wanted to throw the ball in my face instead of trying to score a goal.

My tactics would of course depend upon what team we were playing and how good they were, not to mention the disposition of the hole man. With lesser teams I didn't bother anyone. But with better or equal teams, it was Game On. If I thought I could get to you, I would try to find out how. The guys I couldn't disturb, I'd just gently push them further out than their normal playing depth to gain an advantage for myself.

With the ones I could get to, I usually started with just splashing water over their heads, maybe pushing them with my foot—it was incredible how getting into somebody's personal space was so upsetting to some people. But one of the most effective techniques was just talking to them, especially about their girlfriends and sisters.

With everything unfolding as it did, making observations about people in and out of the water, it became apparent that I had the ability to get inside people's heads. Once I got into their heads, I could make them forget about what they were supposed to be focused on and shift their attention to something that was not germane to the task at hand.

What I discovered was that: *In sports, if you get inside someone's head, you own them. But it works both ways.*

And that was the beginning of understanding something even more fundamental: *There's a focal point. There's something that you're actually supposed to be doing. If you get distracted for whatever reason, if you lose focus, then you're not going to be successful.*

By being the distraction, I could see both sides of the coin, both perspectives. Then the next question to answer was: *Well, how do you* maintain *your focus?*

CHAPTER TEN

Intensity of focus was a new concept for me. Nobody had ever discussed it. When I was competing in swim meets, it wasn't something anybody had made me aware of. Nobody had ever explained anything beyond, "Go do more laps." Even with surfing, I was still working mostly on reflex and instinct.

Once I had discovered that I could distract someone from their objective, and then went on to figure out that I had to develop a method of keeping my own objective in sight—*maintain focus*—it was difficult to get much further with it at first.

The next step was what today we would call prioritizing. For me, it was the beginning of consciously understanding that there even *was* a priority. My priority in water polo was to create a distraction so that somebody would get pissed at me to the point where he'd rather throw the ball in my face than try to score. It was absolutely amazing to see how easily people could be distracted, as well as how a focused and goal-oriented person is very difficult to get off-task.

I started to apply this insight to other areas of my life, thinking about what was most important to me and putting my goals in order to find a path to achieving everything I wanted to achieve. Again, when you don't know anything about a concept or a philosophy and nobody's ever discussed it with you, it has ramifications, because you start applying it in your life in whichever way makes sense to you at the time.

Unfortunately, when I started prioritizing, classwork kept turning up at the bottom of the list. I was much more interested in having a good time. I just wasn't mature enough to be plugged into that particular thing at that time.

Surfing and water polo were neck and neck at the top of the list, with making art and money close behind. Ever since junior high school, I'd enjoyed creating visual art—from the tactile pleasure of sculpting with clay and wax, to the freedom of abstract painting. And I'd loved the concept of making something from nothing all of my life.

Art and money came together my first year at Chabot when a friend of mine made a connection with an art gallery in New York City. We would get all these canvases prepped and spread them throughout his apartment—down the hall, into the bedroom, into the living room. We'd put up a hundred-plus canvases, and the objective was to find anything we could think of to put on them. We did watercolors, oils, and spray paint, but the fun thing was coming up with bizarre stuff. For example, we'd take coffee grounds and spread them on the canvas to get this sort of beautiful organic brown.

The gallery bought everything we produced. We'd take our abstract color art and ship it off to New York and then a check would come back and we'd do it all over again.

Once I was in motion, it was really fun to watch what evolved. Sometimes it was really cool and I'd get very excited about it, and sometimes it just didn't click for me. Then again, something that didn't click for me might click for someone else. That's the awesome thing about art: everybody has a different perspective.

When a piece of art I'd created was off, I just had to take a chill, think it through, and figure out what I did that wasn't pleasing to me and how I could correct it. Then I'd get on a run and everything would be totally awesome again.

It was like what my mother had taught me with watching clouds—*Take a moment to catch your breath and see what's really going on.* Creating art was all about passion and emotion, but I could still control and improve it little by little.

Applying this to surfing and water polo, and to my life in general, I could see how it related to learning to stall the board, or *not* taking out a guy's teeth in the pool. I knew that it had something to do with calmness, being fast without being in a rush, but the connection was elusive. I mean, I was nineteen, and still in a massive rush to who knows where.

Another thing I learned about art is what's called positive and negative space. Positive space is the actual creation of material, whatever material there is, while negative space is the absence of material. Both have to work in balance with each other, whatever balance the artist is trying to create. That may mean the balance is really skewed, as in a 90-to-10 percent ratio, or that may mean a perfect 50-50 balance. It's that perspective of, "They both count, and how do you want to create what you see and what you don't see?"

So I took what I'd learned about focus and prioritizing and added the concept of balance to the mix. That could have led me to reason that with so many hours in a day, there had to be room to accommodate the pool, the ocean, and the classroom—especially since the classroom was the only thing making water polo and surfing possible. (The Vietnam War was in full swing, and I'd be eligible for the draft the second I lost my student exemption.)

CHAPTER ELEVEN

Willie Mays came to San Francisco and played for the Giants when I was a kid. He was the talk of the town, and what the commentators always talked about was how he moved. He was one of those people who spent so much time learning how to do what he did that he reached a point where it became effortless. People like that—they glide. There's an economy of movement to them that makes them very unique. Their understanding of a sport, their understanding of what they are doing and where their head is—the thought that they give to it along with all their athletic ability—gives them an efficiency that makes them surpass what normal athletes ever achieve.

For me, the keystone to that mental process was found in a book called *Psycho-Cybernetics* by Dr. Maxwell Maltz that I came across when water polo season ended and swim season was underway late in my freshman year. It was about what the mind is capable of when faced with a multitude of circumstances. I focused on the section about a technique called visualization that some American prisoners of war had used in World War II. Like any healthy young man in 1968, war was very much on my mind. I knew guys from Hayward and San Francisco who had been killed in Vietnam, and my poor attendance record had already earned me one probation letter from the dean, making expulsion an all too real possibility.

The POWs Maltz was writing about had been held for eighteen months and more, and, during their captivity, they developed the ability to get away from the horrors of the camp by going somewhere else in their minds. One of the places that some of these guys went to was a golf course. Every hole, water hazard, and sand trap was laid out in their minds' eye and they would go there mentally, playing through all of the action stroke by stroke, going through the game detail by detail.

When the POWs were finally sent home and brought back to health, they found out that the better they had been at visualization, the better they were at actually playing golf when they returned to the course. They hadn't played in years and had gone through physical and mental torture, but they were only a couple of strokes over what their handicaps had been before the war. Some of them even played as well as before.

That was fascinating to me. Almost all of the thought I'd given to sports until then had been while I was performing. Visualization was different. It required me to think of something I wanted to achieve and then concentrate on it somewhere other than the water.

The next time I was in the locker room, I went to the chalkboard and posted what my next time for the 200-yard individual medley was going to be. I had decided that I was going to shave ten seconds off my best.

Coach Brown asked, "What's this on my chalkboard?"

"That's my time. I'm going to knock ten seconds off."

"That's ridiculous," he said.

"No," I told him. "In my mind this is what I can do, and I figured out how I can do it. I read this book. It's all there. I got it."

"If you say so. Let's see if you can pull it off."

Following the book, I saw that I had to think about what I wanted to do as a whole, and then break the whole down into small, achievable elements. Then I had to visualize, imagine myself performing each element. By working through that process, I was training my mind and body to perform each component together.

The 200-yard medley consists of the four strokes—butterfly, backstroke, breaststroke, and freestyle—fifty yards each, two laps per stroke in the short course, 25-yard pool. Since I first needed to approach it as a mental exercise, independent of a physical workout, I went home to my bedroom after practice and focused on each element and aspect of a lap, each stroke. I tried to fully imagine how each of them felt, the sensation of the water flowing around my hand and fingers. I concentrated on where my hand was in relation to my chest, paid attention to the angle of my wrists.

Then I thought about what was happening with my breathing, how I always died at the end of butterfly, which was the first stroke in the medley, and how that messed up my time going into the back stroke. I slowed down my breathing, felt the power of my arms pulling me through the water.

Once I started training my mind to create all these mental images, I fully believed my body would recreate them when I wanted it to—as long as I didn't slack on my physical workout either.

The day of the next meet, I separated myself from the team, found a quiet place to focus, and previewed the whole race in my mind one more time. Then I remember the explosion of the starting gun, leaping off the blocks, and gliding underwater dolphin-kicking my legs. This time, I knew exactly how to control my breathing during the butterfly laps because I'd done it a dozen times at home already and once in the locker room right before the race. I never even had to look at where I was in relation to the other swimmers. The only thing I had to do was watch the wall ahead of me coming ever closer.

By the time I reached the wall for the last time, I was so exhausted that all I could do was float. I felt like I'd gone faster than ever, but I didn't know yet if my experiment had worked, busy as I was getting my lungs filled back up.

When I got out of the pool and looked over to Coach Brown, he was smiling. He held up eight fingers. Okay, I hadn't dropped the whole ten seconds, but eight was huge in itself. I could hardly believe it. I thought, "This thing *works!*"

As far as physical preparation went, I hadn't done anything differently—it was the same workout, same everything. It was all the visualization. Shaving those eight seconds made me want to study the technique and better understand it.

For surfing, I started to visualize what was going on by looking at magazines. The pictures showed me what the athletes at the elite levels of surfing looked like as they pulled off their maneuvers, and I was trying to make those connections for myself. What I found was that I could not be in the water and try to make improvements. All I could do when I was in the water was surf. What I needed to do was go back to someplace quiet—my bedroom again, or the living room if nobody was around—and then visualize what I was trying to create.

So, realizing that for an athlete to do something successfully, he or she need only think about it properly when they're not practicing, was an important next step in the process. When it's time to perform, translating thought into physical movement takes a tenth of a second—so *if you're thinking, you're already behind.* Prethinking and preparing everything ahead of time is crucial, so that the body can take over during competition.

I moved into establishing my visual prompts. In surfing, you don't think about what you're going to do while you're doing it, and the carryover is the same for every other sport. If you've prepared through visualization, when you see something happen during your performance, you'll react automatically. If you're a baseball player, you're watching the pitcher's arm and hand movement—that's the prompt you react to. You don't think about what the pitcher is doing; you've seen it enough times that you know and can react accordingly without premeditation.

The aspect of visualization that most fascinated me was getting my mind to be able to reenact a physical movement. When I got really good at doing that, I started visualizing changes to what my physical movement would be. The idea is that you get your muscles involved as you're doing this. It becomes very sophisticated to take it from a mental image that you create to getting a muscular response. When you reach that stage, you can actually be out of the water and still have a surfing experience. It just depends upon the level of sophistication you take it to.

With a lot of work, you can have an actual athletic experience through the process of visualization.

It was only at this point that I began to see that surfing could be art just like Willie Mays made baseball an art. Sometimes with the surfing that I did, I'd know it was clicking; other times, I'd be struggling—it would be like I was playing a guitar but I couldn't get my fingers on the strings exactly the right way to hit the chord. I knew I had to play with it for a while and try to figure out how to get what I wanted. When I hit the right chord, I'd know it.

Most people surfed just like everybody else. The true experts in the surf magazines, though, they had style. They didn't even need good surf because their presentation was so brilliant. For them, surfing was more of a dance than a sport. It was an artistic expression because it had an interpretive value. Yes, athletically there was a lot going on, but the end result was a visual display with a flow, a carryover of movement and motion that used the wave to express itself in a fundamental way.

With this new tool of visualization, I saw that it was possible for me to become an artist with waves—to develop a style all my own. That was going to take a lot of work and a lot of hours at the beach, so I started putting in more and more of them. Of course, those were hours that I wasn't putting into my classes, and the college was only going to put up with a certain amount of crap from a budding young artist.

Much the same could be said for the draft board.

CHAPTER TWELVE

In my second fall quarter I was kicked out of community college, having received a letter from the dean stating that not only wasn't I eligible to swim or play water polo anymore, but that I had managed to fail so many classes that I couldn't even attend school any more. I went straight to the dean with a litany of excuses—my mom was sick, my dad was still recovering from his stroke, I had all these things I had to do. Eventually, the dean decided to be compassionate and said, "Well, okay, I'll give you another shot."

The problem was, it kept happening. I never really accepted what the letters said because I knew what I wanted to do—swim and play water polo. So they would expel me, and I would talk my way back in again and again. After that first talk with the dean, I drifted in and out of school for another two years. It was during one of my off-cycles that my number came up with Selective Service.

The draft was in full effect, and if you were not in school, you were eligible. They had a lottery system where they selected draftees by their birthdays. There were 365 potential selections, and when in December 1969 they held the first national draft lottery since World War II, they drew 195 winning birthdays. Mine was number six.

I had been in the kitchen washing dishes when my sister started screaming in the living room. The lottery was televised, but I didn't watch it because I just thought, "I'll be at the end; I'm not worried."

When I ran into the living room and Cindy told me they'd called my number, I said, "That's not possible. You screwed it up somehow. I'll be fine."

But I was not fine. I was flabbergasted. I'd known that I was eligible, but somehow I just assumed that it would work itself out, or that I'd go back to college before I got called up. Now I was going to get a notice from the draft board telling me when to report for basic training in the Army. I'd seen it happen to a lot of my friends, and some of them were dead, so I knew that basic training automatically meant Vietnam unless I found some way to circumvent it.

I thought of my friends who had never come home again. I had seen their brothers and sisters, mothers and fathers walking around empty and in shock. I had seen guys I knew come back missing hands, feet, legs. When you looked into their eyes, something was missing. They were vacant, lost. Often, they couldn't look you in the eye at all. I didn't even want to think about what they had gone through.

My buddy Bob Pearson wasn't at risk of being drafted since he'd moved on to Cal State Hayward and was doing fine there, but I figured he'd want to have a contingency set up in case school didn't work out or they called his number after he graduated. It's not that as surfers we were automatically hippies or part of the counterculture movement in San Francisco; but, as a kid in 1969, you didn't need to have anything to do with that scene to want to stay out of Vietnam.

So I told Bob, "I know this guy who has a connection over at the Alameda Naval Station. If we go see him, he'll get us signed up with the Marine Reserves." I knew a guy who had done just that, and all he had had to do to fulfill his military obligation was to go to Puerto Rico for two weeks of exercises every year.

"Okay, cool," Bob said.

We had the appointment set with my connection at Alameda, and Bob was supposed to come by and pick me up. Then an hour after he was supposed to come get me, I called him and he just said, "Oh, yeah, well, that didn't work out. How about we go surfing?"

"Good idea," I told him. "Let's go surfing."

Somehow I figured something else would come along. What that would be, I didn't know.

My dad was so pissed. He had been so proud that I was going to enlist, even if it was with the Reserves. He'd been stoked. And then Bob showed up with his surfboard and we took off. Dad didn't say anything—he didn't have to.

After that, I just kept blowing everything off and surfing until I got my notice from the draft board telling me when to report. Once you receive that notice, it's done. It's all over with. There was no talking my way out, there was no changing it. You're drafted, you're now part of the Army, you just haven't gone in yet.

The Army was going to induct me on a Monday. I spent the weekend in the Sierra Mountains near Arnold where my mom grew up and went skiing for the first time with a buddy of mine at Bear Valley. I didn't know the first thing about skiing, but I figured if I broke my leg it was no big deal because I was now Army property. What difference would it make?

Monday morning I said my goodbyes, downplaying the emotions that were rushing through me. Whatever was going to happen, I just wanted to get it over with. There were a bunch of guys I knew at the collection point in Hayward. We were loaded onto buses and shipped to the draft facility in the run-down old business section of Oakland.

It was still dark out when we arrived at the squat, two-story draft building a few blocks off the main downtown area. The building was dark, too. There was something especially off-putting about having us show up before they even opened their doors, like they were saying, "Welcome to your new life. You're on our time now." The streets were deserted. There was a cafeteria a few doors down—that was closed, too. The only place with lights on was a little storefront across the street, so I went over to kill some time until the Army was ready to have me.

It turned out to be a draft resistance center run by Quakers. Well, that was pretty interesting. I went in to see what it was about.

They asked me some questions and I told them I wasn't too thrilled about going to Vietnam.

"You have certain rights," the guy told me. "And one of the rights that you have is that you can ask for a physical."

I thought, "Oh, great. Here I am a surfer, a water polo player, and a swimmer, and I'm going to ask for a physical."

When the induction center finally opened, they grouped us all up and asked, "Is there anything any of you would like to have done?"

We were being dealt with by two very professional Army recruitment sergeants.

I raised my hand and said, "I would like to have a physical."

All the guys around me busted out laughing.

It was ridiculous because if you could walk up the stairs they considered you physically capable. I was 21 years old, 6′ 2″ and about 225 pounds. Smartass remarks started coming from all around the room.

There were two guys among us draftees who had chosen to interpret the professional attitude of the Army sergeants as a weakness, which was seriously poor judgment on their part.

They kept interrupting the sergeants and challenging them. They clearly had no idea about the Army or any kind of serious discipline. So, right before our eyes, they became Marines. Just like that.

Two truly hard-looking men stepped into the room wearing very different uniforms than the first two sergeants—Marine Blues.

One of them asked the recruits, "What are your names?"

The rest of us all sensed the change and tensed up immediately. These two poor bastards were still too full of themselves and thought they still had "rights." They each stated their names.

The smaller of the two Marines grinned a very satisfied grin and told them, "Welcome to the Marines, boys. Follow me."

The larger Marine had moved between the two guys and the rest of us, blocking them from ever rejoining the herd. As a student of movement, I have to say, it was very well done. Quickly, a door opened and two more Marines stepped through, one on each side of the doorway, and escorted the two mouthy recruits through the doors. I saw them later that day, sloughed in their chairs, being told, "You will be a grunt in Vietnam in just a few long weeks, boy. We love potty training sissies like you two."

So, clearly, this was not a place to screw around, but I stuck to getting my physical. Buses took everyone away but me. It took a long time to deal with me because I kept telling them I had a right to a physical.

"You can't have a full physical," a medic finally told me, "but you can select something to be done as part of a physical." The guy then eyed me up and down and added, "Do you have some problem we need to know about?"

"Well, my father has a heart condition so I want my heart checked out."

They sent me into a little room to wait. Eventually the medic came back and said, "What we're going to do is check your blood pressure and find out how you're doing."

I started to freak out. Everything was suddenly becoming way too real. The next stop after this little room was basic training, and that only lasted six weeks. After that it was Vietnam, and that could last forever. I had yet to fully confront just exactly how much I did not want to have to kill people. And I definitely didn't want people trying to kill me. It was all totally disturbing.

By the time they checked my blood pressure, it was through the roof. The medic told me to wait there, came back half an hour later, and checked again. I failed again.

"Are you on drugs?" he asked.

"What? No!"

"Are you doing anything illegal? How come you're like this?"

I told him, "I have no idea. You're the one checking my blood pressure—it is what it is."

So the medic watched me for a few seconds, and then he said, "This is the way it works. You're going to stay here for the next two weeks and we're going to take your pressure several times a day, every day. How's that sound to you?"

"Well, as long as you feed me and give me a place to sleep, that sounds good to me."

It turned out to be a test. Since I wasn't objecting to staying there and being checked out for two weeks, he said I could go home and have my blood pressure monitored by my own doctor, who would give the Army the results.

After I had just spent the morning going through all of these heavy goodbyes, now here I was calling my house and telling my dad, "Hey, I'm not drafted yet. I have testing that has to go on. Can you come pick me up?"

"You're kidding me."

"No! I'm not free but I'm not drafted yet."

Then, with my last dime, I called a surf buddy and said, "I'm not drafted and I know there's waves. If you come by the house in an hour we can go surfing."

*   *   *

My dad ended up taking me to his heart specialist, who asked me up front, "Did you do anything to effect the test? Did you take pills or something?"

"No," I said. "I didn't take anything."

What no one knew was that I had started visualizing being in Vietnam. After I'd failed the test the first time, I realized that I could recreate the fear and make it stronger. In my mind, I was imagining being in the jungle and having people trying to kill me—and my family back home with that empty look in their eyes. When I thought about it to the point where I could see the details in my mind, it scared me so badly that my blood pressure went through the roof.

I would ride my bike over to the heart specialist every other afternoon. After having done a lot of these tests we had accumulated enough data that he was actually starting to worry about me.

"You're a healthy young man," he said, "but you have a history. Your uncle died of heart issues and your father has heart issues. You shouldn't be testing this way. I'm going to ask you again if you're doing anything medically to cause these results."

"No," I said. "I'm not taking anything."

"Then I'm really concerned. It's not healthy. I don't know why you're like this, but if this is who and what you are, I will tell you right now that you cannot smoke, you cannot drink, and you need to take your weight down or you'll kill yourself."

I had come in thinking I had everything covered, but just by the expression on his face I could see that the doctor was genuinely worried about me. He was a good guy, and he told me I'd already failed the test too many times to be eligible for service, so I said, "I'll come in for the last two tests and I'll pass them both."

He sat back with a mix of suspicion and confusion on his face, asking, "And how are you going to do that?"

"I've been working on this thing called visualization. I'm learning how to control my body through it."

After I explained to him about Dr. Maltz's book, he said, "Well, that's a very interesting concept, but I'm not sure if I subscribe to it."

Well, *I* did. For the last two tests I sat in his office for ten minutes and just envisioned being in meadows surrounded by spring flowers, looking up at the sky and watching the clouds pass by. I was all warm and comfortable in the sunshine of this very serene setting I had created. Those two tests showed my blood pressure to be well below the normal rate. He was very impressed.

And I was no longer draft eligible. That changed everything for me.

CHAPTER THIRTEEN

With the Army having officially passed on me, I didn't have to keep up the façade of being a college student anymore. I still loved swimming and water polo, but practice and visualization had improved my surfing to the point where I had become much more interested in continuing to get better at it than I was in those other sports. Plus, my dad still wasn't able to work, and I never wanted to be that vulnerable. The kind of work I'd been able to get while still attending school meant getting minimum wage for trekking out to the new highrise district in Oakland to sweep sidewalks and polish doorknobs before dawn so I could make it back to class in Hayward on time. It's not that I thought it was beneath me, but it didn't make sense to me, going to a job where I didn't learn anything so that I could attend classes where I didn't feel like I was learning anything, either. A real job would teach me more. It would also pay much more.

Money had been a major concern for me ever since I saw what had happened to my father. Not earning a wage made you dependent—it made you susceptible to forces beyond your control. I was raised not to let myself become vulnerable if there was anything I could do about it. Again it was: *Have you done everything you can do? Have you given what was right to give?*

Sure, to my parents' way of thinking, staying in school was a huge part of doing all I could do to secure my future. But the way I saw it, my future was already happening, and fast. I needed to get into it *now*—college was not helping on that front. Every generation in my family had been working-class. As far as I was concerned, I was supposed to be working. It was the only way I could be sure of being able to take care of myself.

My first full-time job was helping a guy build a dam on his ranch. Then I got a position with Gillig Bros. Buses of Hayward, learning fiberglass layup and mold-making. From there my boss asked if I wanted to go to work for him in San Jose, building molds and producing pieces for everything from motorcycle gas tanks to fish tanks, from satellite dishes to fiberglass cars.

My mom was not happy about it. She'd always told me to work with my head, not with my hands. Her vision of me was that I would grow up to be a doctor or a lawyer or something like that. Becoming a professional coach would have been cool with her, too, and now even that had fallen by the wayside. The way I saw it, it would still be there when I wanted it; school wasn't going anywhere. In the meantime, my father was devastated at being unable to support his family the way that he wanted to, and he and my mom had always raised me to become capable, competent, and independent. So at least they could be proud that I was stepping up and taking care of myself.

That had always been such an especially important priority with my mother.

* * *

That summer we were living in Fremont in a house that had a garden out back. It was further from the city than the little apartment, but that meant we got a lot more space for the money, and my mother loved gardening. She was growing tomato plants and they still had some new fruit on them when the season turned and it started to get cold.

One time I said, "Mom, that's a bummer because now they won't ripen."

She said, "That's true, but I can still have fried green tomatoes."

"Green tomatoes?" I said. "Mom, are you kidding me?"

So she fixed fried green tomatoes with a little salt and pepper on them and I couldn't believe how good they were.

That was one of her good days. They were becoming fewer and fewer.

She had been going to the hospital at Stanford for testing over the last few months because her headaches had been getting more painful and more frequent. The X-rays showed what the doctors thought was a brain tumor, but they said they couldn't be sure because the images were so grainy. Experimental brain surgery was one option, with three possible outcomes that they presented her with.

"One: the surgery will fail and in your remaining days you will be in the most horrific pain that you have ever experienced or imagined. Two: the surgery will succeed but you will still experience that pain for a few weeks to a couple of years and then get better. Three: we can do the surgery and nothing will change."

At that point, my mother had heard enough.

I came home from work one night and the house was dark. It was very unusual for my mom not to be home, but I just turned on some lights, fixed myself something to eat, and went to bed. As I lay there, though, I started to feel uncomfortable. Mom was always around to greet us when we got home, so I thought she must be having one of her episodes. I got up and went to my parents' room.

What I remember is seeing her and finding the note to my father next to the bed, then checking her pulse and her breathing. I remember that those things happened, but I don't recall the images. Then I remember going back to my bedroom and trying to decide what to do and how to deal with it. I went into the bathroom and tried to think. I went back to my mother and verified again that she was dead.

I called my father. Since he had started drinking again, I knew where to find him. Cheerio's Cocktail Lounge.

"I'll be home in a little bit," he told me. "I'll deal with it."

He came home and called the ambulance and the police and he dealt with everything. All of the activity of removing her body happened, but I isolated myself in my bedroom and tried to sleep. It was just so hard to face that I now had a life in which somebody who was so important to me was no longer physically there. But I never once thought of my mother as gone. The first time you lose someone that important, you really begin to understand that we are more than just a physical presence. I was in shock and beside myself, but I still felt her presence and held onto it.

The way that I express it is that I have another angel looking out for me now.

If you're fortunate enough to interact with a number of people, you hopefully have left an impression on them. Even when you're gone, they knew who you were and they appreciate who you were; you made enough of an impression that there was some value to who you were.

My mother intentionally overdosed on her medication. She knew where she was with her painkiller addiction, she knew how unlikely it was that she would ever be released from the pain, and she made a decision.

I never questioned it.

After the initial shock, my first emotion was relief. I was relieved that my mother no longer had to be in pain. I had seen her suffering so often, and I had always wanted to go to her and say, "What can I do to help? What can I do to make your pain go away?"

But there was nothing I could do—there was nothing anyone could do. I felt so helpless on so many different levels. She was dealing with something that could not be changed. That's the most tragic thing there is. You feel so incapacitated, so inadequate, that you cannot change certain aspects of life. If you are in constant pain and you cannot alter it, that's unfair. That's a raw deal.

I don't think one person's suicide is anyone's business when that person is in as much pain as my mother was. No one should ever have to be in that position to make those decisions. We should have a better life. How dare anyone make a judgment?

Which is why I take such an issue with people who *can* make so many changes about who they are and where they are but refuse to. They have no clue. They stay stuck. They stay in one place, stuck there mentally and physically.

But in most situations, you can change. You can move. You can do something to improve yourself and your situation. You have to be flexible. Your success can only come if you prepare yourself and have the ability to adapt. That comes when you are willing to invest in yourself and accept who you are today while being willing to morph into something better tomorrow.

I'm not saying I understood all of that back then, but I did know that you could change your situation, see new perspectives, and evolve, all because my mother had made a huge impression on me. She taught me to watch clouds, to see that they could be whatever I wanted them to be, to stop and see what was really going on.

She was a very awesome woman. A tremendous human being.

I wasn't prepared to say that she didn't exist anymore, because she absolutely did. She existed for me because of all the things she had helped create and exposed me to.

On the day of her funeral, I went to the beach. My mother didn't have any family left on her side except for her father. Besides him, it was going to be all my father's people at the funeral, and I didn't want to see them. They'd always shrugged off my mother's medical problems and implied that it was all psychosomatic. It's not only that they never helped: they actually made things worse at times. She was allergic to shellfish, and at family gatherings they would say it wasn't true and pressure her to eat some, or sneak some into her meal—then they'd act surprised when she went to the hospital for a week. Going to the funeral with those people would have felt like sharing my mother with them one last time, and I wasn't willing to do that.

So I went and hung out with the ocean and dedicated the day to my mom. I just walked around thinking about her. I built little memorials out of branches and sticks and flowers. It was warm and sunny under the cliffs out of the wind. I remember lying down in the sand and talking to my mom. There wasn't any surf that day.

My father died less than six months later. They said that his heart gave out. I believe that in a couple of ways. My dad had started smoking and drinking again even before my mother's passing. Afterward, he went at it harder still. But it was by no means the return of Big Lucky. He just didn't feel like he had a lot of reason to live. I would say he died of a broken heart.

Once again I chose not to go to the funeral and went to the beach instead. My grandfather—my mother's father—expressed how disappointed he was. I explained to him that I had had enough of my relatives and how they had interacted with my mother. Things heated up quickly. In the end, I told him, "Not only do

I not need them, but if you're going to side with them, then I certainly don't need to have any contact with you, either."

I didn't speak to him for ten years after that.

My sister was upset because she didn't know what she was going to do.

"Look, I'm the one who cut off the family," I said. "You're younger, you need their support. You should be hanging out with the family. I don't know what I'll be doing or where I'm going."

My father had known lots of people. While I was growing up, one of his rules for me had been, "You're gonna be who you want to be, you're gonna chose to do what you want to do, but, if I need to get involved, your life as you know it will forever be altered." It meant that if what I had chosen to do wasn't okay, I was in deep shit. Being a young man I had contemplated how far away I would have to go to get into mischief without my father hearing about it. To get there and back would have taken so long and would have been so complicated that it was much easier just being good.

Now I could do anything I wanted—go anywhere I wanted.

I decided I would get married and move to the mountains.

PART III
INTO THE MOUNTAINS

CHAPTER FOURTEEN

I'd been told by the people I was working for on the fiberglass job that I'd be out of work for the winter and that I needed to make alternative plans. Well, ever since I'd tried skiing that weekend before I reported for the draft, I'd wanted to get better at it. I figured that since I had a little bank set aside and unemployment would be coming in, it was a great time to move up to Lake Tahoe for a few months and learn how to ski.

What helped in making that decision was that surfing had become very territorial and aggressive in Santa Cruz. I don't know if it was because the sixties were over and everything had gotten just a little uglier, or if a lot of the guys had just reached that age when they start thinking they're too badass. But I'd go surfing in town and suddenly people wanted to verbalize all this bullshit about, "You don't live on this street, man!" They'd be puffing up their chests and yelling and screaming, "This isn't your break! You don't belong here!"

I'd finally had enough when I was surfing at Stockton Avenue one day and a local guy paddled up and told me right to my face, "Get out of the water."

I was like, "*Really*? You and what army? Because it ain't gonna be just you."

From there it was all shouting and cursing, waving our hands in each other's faces and seeing who would be the one to take it up a level. All the while the rest of his crew was paddling up closer because, if either one of us threw a punch, they were all going to jump in. In the end we both backed off and just tried to stay away from each other; but it was a crappy feeling to have that kind of negative energy bringing down my surfing experience—not to mention the possibility of getting piled on in the surf.

Most people would never actually get physical in the water, but there were a few who definitely would. The guy who'd told me to get out of the water had been designated by his group to see if I could be intimidated. Other crews, though, they'd just come on over and start pummeling you—*then* they'd tell you to get out.

I wasn't interested in any of that. I wanted to go surf. I wanted to have a good time. I started surfing up the coast around San Francisco more often because it was more isolated than Santa Cruz. With San Francisco having world-class waves and almost nobody around, there was little reason to deal with the surf jerks at Santa Cruz. It was just going to get me in trouble. I had no issue surfing up the coast, but it's much more fickle and exposed to the elements compared to Santa Cruz, which is inside a bay. Plus, San Francisco took a lot longer to get to, so I was getting less surf time. And I still had no idea at this point that Mavericks even existed.

It seemed like a good idea to change pace for the winter and try something new. And Lake Tahoe definitely seemed like an awesome place to honeymoon.

First, of course, I needed to get married. Diane and I had met at a college dance a couple years earlier and had been going steady for a few months. She was also one of the girls who would come down and hang out at Cull Canyon when I was lifeguarding. French-Portuguese from the Hawaiian island of Maui, Diane had perfect dark skin and hair, with beautiful, large dark eyes. She was somebody who was intelligent, who could think, and with whom I had really good conversations. I figured that if you took two people who seemed to have the compatibility that we did, well, "This ought to work."

I was so clueless. I had no idea. Young, numb, and dumb as ever, I decided that getting married was a good idea. My parents were gone, I was what people back then considered marrying age, and I was in a hurry to start the rest of my life. Getting married was what men did.

Diane was Catholic and I was raised as a Southern Baptist, but at this point in my life I had already developed a more universal belief system. Diane and her family were insistent that we get married in a Catholic church, though. In order to do that we had to go meet the priest and tell him we would raise our kids Catholic. He was a totally cool, well-traveled young man who'd just gotten back from doing missionary work in Africa. Diane had not been attending church regularly and he was upset about that.

"If you two want to get married, you have to participate in church," he said. "You have to go to church on Sundays." Then he turned to me. "If you're going to marry her, it has to be done in the church, and that means that you have to become a Catholic."

"Okay," I said. "Well, that's not happening."

"Well, I need you to tell me that that's what you're going to do."

"I'm not gonna tell you what I'm going to do if that's not what I'm going to do," I said. "I'm just being honest here."

He countered with, "Then we have to have an agreement that when you have kids you will raise them as Catholics."

Back then I wasn't the shining example of tact and diplomacy that I am today. I told the priest, "Well, I'm not going to do that either. Here's where we are: I believe that there's a God, not necessarily *your* God, but *a* God. There is a universal force that I believe in. And I also think that churches suck. It's just a way to collect money. You guys are running a scam."

Had he been older, more traditional, or as much of a hardhead as I was, I don't know what would have happened. But he was from the same generation as Diane and me, and much more from the help-the-people branch of the church than the heavy dogma division. He let us off with my promise to raise the kids with an acknowledgment that there was a God and that I would continue to be respectful and honor my perception of God.

We were married in the big Catholic church in Old Town Hayward. The reception was at Diane's mom's house, hanging out and partying with lots of family around.

The next morning we took off for the mountains.

CHAPTER FIFTEEN

We left in a funky, old, white midsize Oldsmobile station wagon that I'd purchased as a mechanic's special. It was raining and I had no clue about driving in the mountains. I figured the rain was no big deal—I knew how to drive. The car was loaded down and by the time we got to the base of the foothills of the Sierras it was a torrential downpour. Then we started up and the rain turned into snow, coming down hard and ugly. Nobody stopped us to tell us to put chains on the tires but they were closing the road behind us. It just took forever to make any progress.

Our driving directions said our house was three miles past "the big tree," and, when I'd asked how I'd know which big tree I was looking for in the mountains, I was told, "Oh, you'll see it."

Well, it was impossible to see in the snow, but when we got up the mountain, there was an enormous tree smack in the middle of the road. I loved it. We had a tiny furnished wood cabin that was just sturdy enough to keep the snow out, but we didn't need anything more than that. It had a downstairs with a kitchen area, a living room, and an iron wood-burning stove that threw out so much heat once it got going that we had to open the front door to cool the place down even though we'd arrived in the middle of a snowstorm. The bedroom was upstairs and we could only get to it by a staircase that ran along the outside of the house. It was perfect for us.

That first night, I woke up in the dark and thought, "Something's different. Something isn't right. What's going on?"

I listened and listened and I couldn't hear a thing. So I got out of bed and opened a window and looked outside. It was snowing and there was no sound. That's when I knew what people mean by "The silence is deafening." I had to reorient myself. Everything was covered in white. Everything. The snow up there is called Sierra Cement because it has a higher water content than most snow, having just come off the Pacific Ocean. It sticks to everything, and as long as it's coming down and layering up, it creates a blanket that absorbs every sound.

When the sun came out in the morning, though, it was brilliantly whiter than white. Stepping outside in my shorts and flip-flops, I had to cover my eyes. The storm system had passed, the sky was bright blue, and the snow just popped. The first thing I began to hear was the tweeting of all the little birds. They had burrowed into the snow and now they were coming out chirping. Everything had hunkered down under the heavy silence of the storm. Now I was seeing and hearing a rebirthing process. Everything was so alive and so vibrant.

I was excited to start skiing, but I also knew this was one of those times to just slow down enough to be able to see and hear and absorb what was going on around me. It was vivid blue and white and I could feel the heat of the sun coming off the snow through the crisp, cold air. When I closed my eyes, I could hear the crackle of the snow melting down through its own depth and moving across the ground. It was winter on a mountainside and I was dressed for the beach, but I felt completely warm.

* * *

As was my style, I had already bought boots and skis because I believed that if you wanted to do something you just jumped in and did it. The house was at the base of a hill so I walked around until I found a road that wasn't too steep. Since I didn't know how to ski, I figured all I needed was a clear surface with some snow on it. I started polling along to get some momentum and just acclimate myself to the feeling of being in skis. From there I went to a more steeply sloped area where I starting building little ramps for myself. It got boring pretty fast, so I decided I might as well go to the ski resort at Alpine Meadows and start to figure out how I was going to do this.

I was so new to the experience that I didn't even know what to ask, which is what I told the pro at the ski shop. He explained to me that most of the locals bought season passes that were good except on weekends. It was cheap enough that even Diane and I could afford it. Diane also splurged on skiing lessons, but I found a way around that for myself.

I quickly went through the bunny slope and moved onto the intermediate slopes. There were instructors giving lessons to groups and individuals all down the slopes. Skiing straight down was easy enough, but I didn't know how to turn or stop, so I became very good at falling down. That made sense to me from surfing: *When you're experimenting and trying to learn, you're going to fall—when you stop falling, you start stagnating.*

When I fell down near people who were getting lessons, I'd carefully listen in to find out if the instructor was saying anything that was pertinent to me. I tried to fall near people who were getting individual lessons as opposed to groups, figuring that they would be progressing much faster. But all the instructors seemed to be teaching the same thing: the snowplow technique. That was where you stand facing downhill and create a V-shape, with the tips of your skis being closer together than the tails. The idea is that, by pushing the skis outward, you weight the inside edges and it stops you from going anywhere. Then, as you lean one way or the other, it takes the weight off one of the edges and puts it on the other and you start to turn. It seemed like a really stupid technique, slowly and awkwardly creeping downhill, and a very inefficient way to learn how to stop and turn. But I didn't know anything else, so I listened, without a lot of success.

I knew it was an intermediate step, but I would just as soon move onto whatever was beyond it.

Halfway down the intermediate slope, I fell by somebody who was teaching a technique that seemed logical to me, which was to ditch the V-stance and put my feet close together, weighting the front, middle, or tail on the edges and using physics to get the skis to bend. That body position reflected the neutral athletic stance I was so comfortable with from surfing—balanced, relaxed, and slightly flexed for control and power.

Then I understood that it was actually a speed and directional control mechanism. That made perfect sense to me. I got back up and skied a little bit further with this new knowledge. It totally worked. So I went to the bottom, came back up, and fell by the same instructor again to pick up a little more.

Once I could identify the instructors who gave out information that I could work with, I would keep falling by them to listen because, when you don't have any skills, when you're at the very beginning of learning something, you need to learn everything and you can only relate to so much. Your capacity to absorb information is relatively limited because, even though you're hearing the words, you can't understand what's being said without a point of reference. That's why listening and receiving coaching becomes so critical to one's progression. By merely listening to two knowledgeable and experienced people converse, you can learn so much. You may not be able to relate to a lot of that conversation because it's not in your bank of references, but just being around people and listening is how you start to acquire those references.

You need a strong data bank of information to draw from, but you can't just listen and not do. So there is listening and then trying to visualize what they're saying, putting a mental picture in your head, and then there is actually doing it physically. Because it's physical, you have all these moving parts—arms, legs, knees, hips, head, shoulders. One of the things that really good athletes understand is that you have to isolate those parts and go back to basics. Every sport has all its own movement idiosyncrasies.

This is where the complexity really comes to the forefront. As a beginning skier, I didn't know anything, so I had to go through much and more of this exposure, incorporating how to use my feet, how to use my knees, what was happening with my hips, why my shoulders needed to be pointed in a certain direction. That began the process. I loved the process, and I loved improving.

I was happy because I was progressing at what I thought was a reasonable rate. There was still nothing like surfing, but skiing, gliding across a mountain—that kind of speed was a way cool thing, all the energy in that motion. The faster I went, the better it was, especially once I had a little bit of control and learned how to turn and stop. It was incredibly freeing. There was no mechanical means, no engine grinding, and, as I'd build up speed to about twenty miles an hour, I'd begin to hear the sound of the wind streaming past my ears. It was a whole new kind of blast to be able to move that fast without expending a lot of energy.

Going up on the lift and seeing all the different exposures of the mountainside, I knew I was out in the wild and I would look around and smile. When I would start my run down the mountain, with my body doing the correct and proper controlled movements to regulate where I was going and how fast, it was breath-taking. It was very close to flying. I was free.

When I finished out that first season, I had some competency and was cautiously moving on to the advanced slopes. I still fell a lot, and not on purpose. I knew that I wasn't such an exceptionally gifted athlete that I could just look at something and get it. I had to look at it, begin the process of experimentation, and try to figure out if I was really getting it or not. I had to look at what the parameters were as far as being successful or not. That required a lot of falling.

But it was spring and down by the Pacific, the surf was up. When we'd moved up to Tahoe I had fully expected to go back to my waves and my job in San Jose after the winter. No one was more surprised than me when Diane and I decided to stay in the mountains indefinitely.

CHAPTER SIXTEEN

It was God's country. Everything just said, *Yes!*

I would take the dog, drive toward one of the ridges on the west side of the lake, and then hike over the ridge. From there I had hundreds of miles of seemingly endless vistas open to me. On a clear day I could see Mount Diablo 160 miles away near San Francisco Bay. I could walk forever and not see any signs of another human being.

Being in the mountains I just felt so close to the universal spirit—so alive. I'd walk around and see mountain lion prints, bear prints, coyotes. When you are walking around in the mountains you are just as big as you can be. You don't have anything to worry about—there's no one around (I was never worried about the animals). So I would leave Friday night or Saturday morning and come back on Sunday, just hiking around and absorbing it all. I slept wherever I laid down my sleeping bag.

The only thing I had to worry about was money. Since the plan had been to move back to the city and return to my job at the fiberglass tool and dye shop in the spring, our small savings were running out, along with my unemployment checks.

Throughout the winter, I'd been getting to know a bunch of people and making friends, so I knew that there was going to be a lot of building going on. Some of the guys I skied with told me that the local construction companies did their hiring in the spring for projects that lasted through the fall, then they would shut down when it started to snow and everyone would spend the winter skiing.

Union laborers were getting six dollars an hour plus benefits and paid vacation. I was all over that deal. I drove into Truckee where the laborers' union hall was. They agreed to let me pay off the union fee of $400 on an installment plan, and the dispatcher told me, "All you need to do is get a shave and a haircut and we'll send you out."

Of course I had no intention of shaving or cutting my hair. When I went on down to the job site, the foreman looked at me and said, "You're not here to go to work."

"Yeah I am."

"Not with that hair and that beard you're not."

Oh my God, I thought. He's serious!

It was a real easy decision. I went home, just stuck my fingers in my hair and started snipping everything off. I shaved everything but my mustache and went back to the job site.

"You don't listen very well," the foreman told me. "You're probably not going to work out."

"No, no," I told him. "I was just hoping."

"There's no hoping. I was very clear."

I said I'd be back in half an hour without the mustache. On the one hand, I was pissed because he dared to tell me how I could look? But on the other hand, he was the guy with the job.

Once I got to work, I realized I knew nothing. I didn't even know what a two-by-four was. At first it was no big deal because all I was doing was digging ditches. Then we started pouring concrete patios to finish up some condos and, after that, we moved into the framing stage of a new development that was just going up. There was a forklift on site, the idea being to keep all the building pad areas fully stocked so that the carpenters could work nonstop. My job was make sure they had what they needed. If the carpenters stop working, they get upset because a good supervisor is watching to see who is productive and who isn't. And if you're not productive on a construction site, you're gone.

One of the carpenters told me, "We're going to need four boxes of sixteens throughout the day." I had no idea what that meant.

I told the carpenters, "You show me one of whatever it is you want me to get and then I'll take care of you."

They showed me that a sixteen was a type of nail. Because I had committed to the mountain and becoming a good skier, I had decided that I needed to be in *really* good shape. I'd stopped using the car, got an old girl's Schwinn, and I would bike or run up and down hills all day long. So when they asked for four boxes of nails I figured I'd do it in one trip. When I got back to the building pad, the guys were staring at me.

One of them said, "Dude, what's your deal?"

"I don't know what you mean."

"Do you know how much weight you have?"

"Well," I said, "you asked for four boxes, so I got you four boxes."

"Each of those boxes are a keg of nails, and they weigh fifty pounds each."

I said, "Yeah?"

"You're *ours*," he told me. "You see us every morning. We'll take care of training you. Don't worry about a thing."

I found that if I talked to the forklift guy early in the afternoon about what my guys would need the next morning, he'd make sure my site was stocked and my guys would never run out of supplies. Meanwhile, I began to learn the process of construction.

Toward the end of the summer I was watching a carpenter and his partner. I was very aware that carpenters made twelve dollars an hour, which was twice my pay, and I saw the carpenter call to his partner, "Hey Bill, cut me a block—ten and thirteen of the little marks."

The guy was making double my pay and he didn't know that "the little marks" were sixteenths of an inch. That was a big part of his job—to quickly and accurately take and give measurements—and he barely knew how to read a tape.

At the end of the day I went to the head carpenter and said, "You see that guy over there? I want his job."

He laughed. "Well, what makes you think you can do his job?"

"He makes twelve dollars an hour and he can't read a tape. By tomorrow morning, I'll be able to read a tape. I want that job."

He just laughed again and said, "You're really funny."

"No man, I'm serious. Construction is cool, I'm having a blast. But he's making twice as much money as I am, and it doesn't take a genius to figure out that twice as much money is way cooler."

"Well, you don't just walk in and become a carpenter," he said. "There's a reason they get paid more."

The next morning, I went back and told him, "I can read a tape. I'm ready to take that guy's job."

Shaking his head, he said, "I'll tell you what, kid. I'm going to do you a favor. I'm going to send you down to the carpenters' union hall and if they'll accept you as a carpenter's apprentice and dispatch you back out here to me, you will do everything you've been doing up until now, but for less money. Then you can start learning to be a carpenter. But you're going to work for a year or a year and a half for less than you're making right now."

"Well, how long do you have to be a carpenter's apprentice?"

"Four years."

"Are you *kidding* me? That's forever!"

"That's the deal."

Down at the carpenters' hall they told me that, since I was already in construction, they would waive the probation period and let me start at the next level, which meant that I'd get a raise in three months and be back to earning what I'd made as a laborer. After that, I'd get a raise every quarter until I was making $12 an hour in four years. I spent a few more weeks doing laborer's work, and then they shut the project down for the winter.

Everyone knew that had been coming, and we'd all been saving up our money. I had purchased new skis and boots and my season pass. It started snowing and I started skiing again.

For the people who lived in the mountains it was really amusing to watch all the people who came from the Bay area on the weekends and spent a lot of money on their outfits when they should have been spending it on ski lessons because they couldn't ski. We always said, *If you're all into style but you've got no skillage, what's the point?*

We were always interested in getting really good equipment and we could care less about what we wore. Hell, I skied in a wetsuit with coveralls and a sweater.

A few weeks in, though, I snapped a pole on one of the advanced slopes. I wasn't going to stop skiing but I didn't know what to do. Then this guy saw me standing there, staring at the remains of my pole, and he said, "You know what? You don't need poles anyway. They're just a timing technique."

I was like, "Dude, I think you're crazy. Everyone else has got poles."

"No, this is going to be perfect. I haven't worked on my timing technique for my hands and arms in a long time. I'll teach you how to do it without poles."

What he taught me was that I had snapped the pole in the first place because I'd become pole-dependent and was putting too much weight on them to make my turns. We went up to the top of this run and he tossed his poles behind a tree. Then he showed me how to use my upper body to go through all the motions as if I were planting a pole, but to just flick my body to one side without ever actually having anything in my hands. It was really all about how you used your shoulders, hips, knees, and feet, and how you set everything up. By simply reaching out I could change the weighting and unweighting through the use of my upper body. It worked beautifully. It completely changed how I skied.

What was even cooler was the fact that a perfect stranger had stopped and taken the time to teach me how to get better at something. He had nothing to gain from it except maybe karma or feeling good about helping out a fellow human being. That kind of mindset had not been prevalent in surfing at all, especially when Santa Cruz started getting crowded and all the surf jerks started hassling people about where they were from and who was allowed to catch what wave.

I wondered if there was something about the mountain that made people think and act differently, or if it was just this guy. I also wondered how that attitude would go over back at the beach, if I ever got back there. It had been six months since I'd surfed and I didn't miss it.

The guy told me, "I used to be a member of the Squaw Valley Ski Team. I live in Reno and I come here to ski three or four times a week. I'll meet you up here and we can ski together. I enjoy teaching people how to ski."

That invitation was really going above and beyond. Gratefully, I accepted and started working with him. I was progressing really well until I broke my skis and had no means to replace them. It was going to totally screw up my whole situation because I had no extra money in the budget for new skis. I needed a job.

Over at the union hall, they told me that a contractor named Frank Stella Jr. needed a carpenter's apprentice for a job that was just around the corner from my cabin. It sounded perfect to me because I could just roll out of bed at ten to eight, walk up the hill, and after two weeks I could buy some new skis.

When I got to the site the next morning, Frank told me, "First you dig the footing of the house out from under the snow. However long it takes you to dig it out, you do that part for free. When you work as a carpenter, that's when you get paid."

"Well," I said, "that sucks."

Once again I was told, "That's the deal."

It only took a couple hours to dig out the base of the house and start getting paid. That's when I really started pissing people off. I would show up just on time, not a minute early, and I kept taking breaks to go home. When my two weeks were done, I just stopped showing up. I knew the job wasn't over—I mean, I could still hear them working up the hill, but I'd been told two weeks and that's what I gave them. I didn't even say goodbye or anything—I just got my check and went back to skiing.

In the spring I knocked on Frank's door and said, "I'm ready to work."

He laughed in my face. "You gotta be kidding me! You had a job and then you quit."

"Well, I'm ready now."

"Well, I don't have a job for you."

I just nodded and said, "Okay, see you tomorrow."

Every day for more than a month, I'd get to his house in the morning while it was still dark out, and I'd stand there until I saw the lights go on. Frank would come out and I'd say, "I'm ready for my job."

Again and again he told me, "You don't have a job." And every time I'd answer, "Okay, see you tomorrow."

Finally, he shook his head and asked, "Are you going to keep doing this?"

All I could say was, "I want a job."

"All right," Frank said, and laid down the law. "This is how it's going to work. If you can get to the site by 7:45 today, and if the guys will accept you back, you've got a job. But I'm telling you right now—I'm not going to put up with any of your shit."

The job site was the base and the bare, first-floor frame of a house they were building in the lake basin surrounded by evergreen trees. The view of Lake Tahoe was spectacular, the air filled with the scent of evergreen, and I thought that, even with the inevitable rain and freezing snow, it looked like a great place to spend the workday.

I got there early like Frank told me to. The other three guys were even clearer about the situation than he had been. A journeyman named Butch spoke for the crew.

"We will teach you whatever you need to know," he told me. "We're taking time out of our productivity to teach you. Your job is to learn. Ask questions."

I just thought, "Man, I'm back in college. This is just carpentry—how hard can it be?"

"If you disrupt us," Butch warned, "we will remind you by throwing hammers at you."

He was completely serious.

* * *

One of the first things they tried to show me was how to make two pieces of plywood meet in the middle of a stud. I paid no attention. So when I went to do my first one, of course it was completely off.

I called out, "Hey, this doesn't work!" Instantly, two hammers came flying at me.

I dodged the hammers and Butch said, "We explained that to you. It's your job to pay attention and to know what to do."

That night I went home and thought about it. My dad, my mom, Coach Brown—all my life people had been telling me to pay more attention. Now I was twenty-two, married, and it was still happening.

So I finally started paying attention. These men took their jobs very seriously. They took making money for Frank very seriously because they understood that, if they weren't doing a good job, then they weren't making Frank money, and, if Frank wasn't making money, he couldn't keep them employed. Frank took very good care of his people—he always paid over scale. If you weren't good enough to be making him enough money so that he could pay you so generously, he got rid of you. There was no use for dead wood. Either you were really good and he'd pay you for being really good, or you had to get the hell out of there.

That was my introduction into what working was really all about. Up to that point, I thought I had understood what being really good at something meant, but then I realized that I hadn't fully gotten it.

What I was starting to learn was: *If you want to excel at any endeavor, you can't shortcut it.*

For instance, it was expected that I could drive nails. I'd never done that. My solution was that I started taking a bag full of nails and a chunk of wood home every night, driving the nails in again and again until I could drive them straight and quickly every time. I walked around the house measuring things with my tape so I could get really familiar with it, and I tried wearing my carpenter's belt everywhere to break in the stiff leather. That didn't work so well; I ended up using a trick I had learned from my mom when she would break in my new Levi's, letting the bags soak in water until the material expanded and I could get the bags to wrap around my hips.

That winter I didn't ski at all during the week because Frank still had work for us. I was trying to get better at my job, so I had to buy the more expensive weekend ski pass. Butch was the master carpenter on my framing crew when the engine of my 1960 Ford Falcon coupe gave out, so I asked him if he could drive me to work in the mornings until I could get it fixed.

"Yeah, sure," he said, "but here's the deal. I want you waiting outside so I know that you're ready. If you're there, I'll stop and pick you up."

Well, my listening skills still needed refinement, I found out. The next morning was just miserable with the snow, rain, and wind, and I was waiting in the house. I could see Butch coming up the road, so I reached down to grab my tool belt and lunch, opened up the door, started to walk out and Butch just kept on going. I ran down the street waving but he never even looked back. Eventually, I managed to hitch a ride and got to the site on time.

Butch was in the house frame, doing his prep work for the day, when I came up and said, "Butch, you didn't stop and pick me up!"

He just looked at me like I wasn't there, said nothing, and continued to prep and stock for the day. When I finally joined in and started working, he pointed out, "When I drove by, you weren't standing there."

"No, but I was in the house coming out."

"I told you I would pick you up if you were standing there. Were you standing there?"

"No, but—!"

"Were you standing there?"

"Oh."

And so my listening skills improved. I started driving into work with Butch every morning. He was a man of few words, often saying nothing but "Good morning" during the half hour trips. His truck, his rules, so I followed his lead. What he did tell me was to use the ride to think about the day ahead so I'd be ready to work before I got there. I learned to think about the tasks that needed to be done and set a plan for the day.

I adopted Butch's motto: *Think, plan, be ready.*

That was the beginning of my construction career. It was also the beginning of learning to be an adult.

CHAPTER SEVENTEEN

During my third season in the mountains, I was out skiing one day in Squaw Valley when I got together with this guy on the chairlift and he asked where I was going to ski. I told him where I was headed and he said, "Are you open to going somewhere else?"

"Oh, sure."

We went on over to an area I'd never seen before. I'd always stayed within the bounds of what the ski area was. Now he was asking me to ski to the edge of that area and beyond it. It was an awesome day, all sunny and warm. Where we were, the snow had slid off the mountain, leaving just ice behind. He skied down a hundred yards, doing all these fancy turns like it was fresh powder. I'd never skied on ice before. My skis didn't work worth shit. Immediately, I was sliding and slipping and out of control.

When I eventually made it to where my skiing buddy was waiting for me, he said, "Give me your ski."

I looked at him, wondering if I was so bad that he wanted to throw my skis down the mountain. "What do you mean, give you my ski?"

"Take your ski off and give it to me. I need to sharpen the edges."

I handed it to him, he reached into his backpack, pulled out a file, and sharpened my skis right there. I was very impressed.

"You've got to do this several times during the day," he said. "It really gives you precise, defined turning."

With that one tip, this stranger had just added a huge file of ski-maintenance knowledge to my data bank. I'd known nothing about it before. Here was yet another truly capable, confident athlete who wanted nothing more than to share his understanding and love for the sport.

We skied the next section and suddenly I could turn. My edges would hold, they would bite. We were right on the edge of the ski area and I was right on the edge of my abilities. Then he took me to an area that was even steeper, and it was even better.

He told me, "My name's Rick Sylvester. I'm an extreme skier."

We hung out a few more times, and Rick told me about jumping cliffs at Squaw Valley. Somewhere around high school I had developed a fear of heights. Well, here I was in the mountains, going through this process of discovering myself and growing. What better way to get over my fear of heights than to start jumping off cliffs?

There's an area called the Cornices that has drops of anywhere from five feet to fifty or sixty feet. If you do everything right, you drop down and ski away and it's all cool. Once Rick and I started jumping cornices together, I really got into it. At first, I was extremely uncomfortable, but I was doing it anyway. Actually, I was doing it *because* it challenged my comfort zone, which meant I was learning.

All the cells in my body would scream out, "Dude, *really?* We're doing this again?"

Rick and I started jumping together and I learned to be very successful at it, working my way up to fifty- and sixty-foot drops.

Meanwhile, some guys Rick knew were talking to him about doing a ski movie.

Rick said to me, "The opening scene will be these people skiing down and then going off this cornice and they want to do it at night."

"But, Rick," I said, "how can they see what the people are doing at night?"

"Oh, did I forget to tell you? They want to light you on fire!"

They actually got people to do it, but not me.

* * *

That season I learned just how tight the skiing community really was. When you skied at a particular resort there were people you'd meet on the mountain who were very like-minded. It turned out that there was a group of about fifteen people that grew to thirty or forty highly skilled skiers. They moved around the mountain to be on the best snow at any given time as the sun changed conditions in different areas throughout the day. I somehow managed to become part of that group.

The incredible thing was how good these people were. Many were becoming world-class skiers, some had already finished their run of being world-class skiers, and some were among the best professional skiers at the time, chilling on their home turf in between events. You could go skiing with some of best people in the world and, if you asked them, they would help you. Some of these people were in the top twenty skiers in the world, and I got to work with them just by asking.

One of the typical things to do at the end of the day was to gather at the top of Squaw Valley and have a speed run—fastest one down the mountain wins. That's how I learned to speed ski. It was never about winning that race; it was about being together, sharing the sport.

If there was some trick I wanted to learn, I only needed to ask any one of them and they were more than generous with their time and advice. They were very accommodating. They'd take me away from the group and work with me. Everybody at some level was great at something and, if not, you just had to be a nice person. That was the only criterion to get into the club. And if you weren't a nice person, nobody had the time of day for you.

It was really wonderful to see this group of people with no territorial bullshit—no, "You're not from here." There was no hostility or localism. They were willing to accept you for who you were and, what's more, they were willing to take the time to teach you things. And they were experts. They weren't punks who thought they could rock; they were the real thing.

Thinking back to the surf jerks, I realized that when you are great at what you do, you know it. That proficiency, that sense of self, eliminates the ego and fear that turn so many athletes I've seen into childish asses.

I hadn't chased a wave in nearly two years and I hadn't missed it. I hadn't surfed, I hadn't seen the ocean. But at the end of the season in Squaw Valley, something suddenly clicked in my head and announced: "I'm ready to go back to the beach."

PART IV
MAVERICKS

CHAPTER EIGHTEEN

Santa Cruz and San Francisco were only a couple of hours from the mountains, so I spent the spring and summer making the drive down on my days off to get myself acclimated to surfing again. My old friend Bob Pearson had started his own business shaping custom boards, and he had so many orders that he and Doug had opened a surf shop, but aside from them I really didn't try to reconnect with anyone from the old scene at first. Whether I was surfing no-name spots or Steamer Lane, I never worried about the territorial nonsense. Before I got back to the beach, I wondered how that stuff would affect me, if it was still prevalent or not. But as soon as I got in the water my total focus was the waves.

That was important, because I was getting ready for something big. The biggest, in fact. I was twenty-six, more mature and thoughtful now than when I'd last been serious about surfing, so my skillage advanced much more quickly than it ever had before. After a month or so, I decided that I wanted to put it to the ultimate test.

That meant surfing Hawaii. The North Shore of Oahu was the acknowledged big wave mecca, because, once the Pacific swells started coming through in winter, it had more waves of consequence than anywhere else. I hadn't become a big wave rider yet, but that's what I wanted to do. In October, the mountains were just beginning to receive snow, so we were still between seasons. It was a great time to go to Hawaii and surf.

The North Shore was where you went to become acknowledged as a player in the world of big wave riding, and Waimea Bay was where the players' players went to perform at the very top of their game. All the legends went there—Greg Noll, Gerry Lopez, Shaun Tomson, Rabbit Bartholomew, Rory Russell, Mark Richards, Owl Chapman, Derrick Dorner, Mike Miller. When Waimea is on, the waves are anywhere from twenty-five to fifty feet high. In Waimea Bay, there is a bowl of white sand that forms a natural arena where thousands of people gather to watch the action when a swell comes in.

There was no way I was surfing Waimea.

For a California surfer, you started at Steamer Lane, then you went for the bigger surf around San Francisco. After that, when you finally got to Hawaii, you had to start off at Sunset Beach in Haleiwa, or Pipeline off Ehukai Beach in Pupukea, or at the break at Makaha Beach Park. No one starts at Waimea. There's no way to be ready for it until you've done extensive training in the North Shore's smaller waves—which aren't all that small, either.

After you'd done Sunset or the Pipe for a few seasons, *maybe* you could get your ticket punched at Waimea. Then you were as legit as anyone in the world. But I knew there was no shortcutting it, not if I wanted to live to tell the tale.

I knew about the culture because I'd gone to Hawaii for a few weeks in 1969, but I hadn't surfed any large waves then. At the time, I just didn't have the training. I'd also been reading about Hawaii in the surf magazines since I was a teenager.

The difference between regular surfing culture and the culture of big wave surfing is the intensity. I'd been a surfer and hanging out with all types of surfers since it became a fad in the early sixties, when it was all Beach Boys and people strapping boards to their cars just for the look. The guys who went after the monsters, though, they were serious dudes. They could be big-hearted and a total riot, but there was always a powerful intensity to them. You can be passionate about normal surfing, but it's still playful. Big wave surfing is no game.

* * *

It wasn't just the waves that were calling. From everything I knew about Hawaii, Hawaiians truly saw so many great surfers. The neighborhood kids were such experts that, if you thought showing up as a great surfer got you anything, you found out quickly that they just didn't care. If you were a great surfer but you didn't want to participate in getting anything done, you weren't going to last long. Hawaiians did things as a community. And I'd heard that, once you were accepted in, you'd get invited to do all this cool stuff like luaus and hukilaus. You'd be welcomed but you had to bring something, and that was your willingness to be cool and to participate.

It was like our little skiing group, but with clear, warm water and enormous waves thrown into the mix.

Once I landed, I found a lanai—which is just a covered, screened-in patio—to rent in a little neighborhood on the Haleiwa side of Laniakea. Laniakea is not known as a serious wave, but it's a notable wave, and it was great for me to experience. It's the first wave you see when you leave Honolulu and take Kam Highway around the island. When I left Honolulu and headed out of the mountains that first time, I came out on what was then all pineapple fields, looked to the north, and saw this vast, vast, *vast* ocean and all of this breaking white water. As a surfer, I knew exactly where I was because I'd been seeing it in magazines since I was a kid.

As I rode through the pineapple fields and cow pastures and then into Haleiwa, I was jittering.

Hawaii is right in the middle of the Pacific Ocean with no continental shelf, so it's very exposed to the ocean's energy. Once the energy comes off the storms, there's no terracing under the water to slow down the swell. Nothing has harnessed it and it comes at you raw.

Those waves move incredibly quickly. One of the first things you learn if you haven't been to Hawaii before is that, the first time you paddle through a wave, you get ducked back. When you're paddling out to go surfing on, let's say, a head-high day, there's a procedure called a duck dive. You stick the nose of your board below the surface of the water as the wave approaches and you force the nose down; then you weight the back of the board with your knee until you can get it to angle up. The board is suddenly a lot deeper underwater than before and it wants to go to the surface. That happens very quickly because of the board's buoyancy, and you pop up on the back side of the wave and paddle away.

But in Hawaii, the waves move so fast and their back sides are pulling, so if you don't do everything perfectly and start to paddle immediately, you get sucked toward the beach and tossed over from the back side of the wave to the front. You can tell who's new because it happens to everyone. It doesn't happen at your local break, but you hear about it before you even show up on the North Shore. And the first time it happens to you, you go, "Holy shit, it's true!"

The first time for me was at Sunset. My goal was to surf Sunset every day because, while its wave wasn't known for being the largest, it was known as being one of the best, most perfectly shaped. Sunset, for me, was an awesome wave because I noticed right away that here, the water moved like the California waters I was used to.

For success, no matter what sport you're doing, start with something familiar. That way, you put in a strong, solid base and build from there.

With the water at Sunset moving around so similarly to what I was used to, it gave me a higher level of comfort and confidence than I might otherwise have had. On my first session there, it was breaking overhead but only at eight to ten feet. It wasn't double-overhead but overhead that the Hawaiians called Sunset's playful stage.

I took off on a wave and immediately knew I was late. I stood up and right away I got pitched over the lip. What flashed through my mind was that I'd be able to go down, transition from the lip into the flat of the wave with all of that speed behind me, and then be able to lay out the bottom-turn right on the corner of the wave, rocket into the pocket, scoot down a little bit, and get barreled.

The reality was, as I transitioned from the lip into the flat, what I had never experienced before was that the wave drove the lip into the surface of the water and then exploded. So instead of being able to make that transition, I got tossed off my board and my legs split. And it wasn't just my legs. They got so pulled apart in that tumble that my baggies were torn from the front all the way through my legs and around to the back.

My junk was hanging. I got tossed, tumbled, and humbled.

"Oh man," I told myself. "I've got so much to learn. Okay, big boy, time to reassess. Either you go back in or you stay out."

So I tucked my tail between my legs and paddled back out, caught a few smaller waves, reclaimed some pride, and went back to the lanai to lay out and think about what had happened.

I'd never been in a serious barrel for any length of time before. I'd been covered up, but only for a short moment. In surfing lore, if you're in a barrel and the wave crumbles and you don't come out, it doesn't count; if you're in a barrel and you almost come out, that doesn't count, either. You have to pull the whole deal.

In Hawaii there are waves you can ride where you can be in the barrel for a number of seconds, which in surfing is a very extended period of time. That was what going to Hawaii was all about. No matter how good you are, wherever you're from, it's a completely new experience. So even though I'd been outclassed by Sunset, and I knew not to even try the monster waves yet, I was determined to get fully barreled before I went home.

A place I knew of that had a barrel was Rocky Point. I went down there one day and saw that the waves were chest-high to slightly overhead. This place was known for breaking left, which was harder to surf for a regular-foot guy like me. But it also has a right, so I decided to ride the right.

I saw a wave coming, paddled hard, caught it, and stood up. As I went into my crouch, I was watching an aqua-marine tube forming right in front of me, seeing all the curvature that it takes to make a barrel, feeling that energy. I slowed myself down by sticking my hand into the rising, curling water of the wave. All of this was new. It was way mega, beyond my ability to comprehend. I'd been discovering all that, but there was a problem. At the end of the wave, there was a coral head. I was so enthralled by what I was doing that I didn't see the coral head until the last second, and I crushed the nose of my board right into it.

But the barrel was so cool that I just thought, *Oh well*, and paddled back out. I broke off the fiberglass from the bottom of the nose so that I wouldn't strip the entire bottom of the board off, and just kept catching more and more waves. Unfortunately, I also kept smashing the nose of my board. I was too stubborn and too ignorant to turn at the very bottom of the wave. I kept waiting for something else to change so that I could get by that coral head.

At the end of my session I went back to the lanai, cut off six or eight inches from the end of my board, stuck on a new section and reshaped it, then went out and did it again the next day. When I got back from that session, rather than think about another way to surf that wave, I prefabricated a bunch of new noses. It ended up taking another three or four days before I learned that I could actually turn and come out in front of the wave—that it wasn't so powerful that it was going to knock me off.

There were several days on that first trip when there was no surf, so I watched the big wave riders going through their unique brand of training. Big wave riders in Hawaii trained beyond surfing. I'd see them running at the beach and recognize it as something I had used in my own training, but they also did something that I hadn't seen before. They would go someplace where they could swim down deep—all the way to the bottom under twenty or thirty feet of water. Then they would pick up rocks and run along the bottom for a distance. This would get them acclimated to being underwater under tremendous exertion. Because if you're on a big wave and you wipe out, that's what's going to happen. You're going to be underwater and you're going to try to save as much energy as possible, but at some point you're going to have to exert yourself to get back to the surface and breathe. So you have to find a way to be comfortable in such an extreme situation.

I started emulating their training while I still had the warm, clear water available. Being in the water builds a bond and increases your understanding of it. I was picking up all these subtleties and watching all the different currents and seeing the fish change the deeper down I swam. *The more observant you are, over time you begin to build up a real understanding.*

That kind of training felt normal to me because I was so comfortable in the water. It's who I am. It was like going back to being a kid swimming in a lake where I could see underwater and just be free. But it was even better because this was the ocean and I could feel it alive all around me. It was a whole different level from anything I'd experienced before.

Having been a kid reading surf magazines and seeing all the photos, I had picked up information over a long period of time, I knew what was supposed to be going on. Then I got to Hawaii and I could see people doing it. There weren't many people, because big wave surfing still hadn't become popular, but if it was popular anywhere back then, it was Hawaii. The few big wave stars that existed were revered there. Everybody knew who they were. The North Shore isn't a big area, and it had hardly been developed yet, so it was easy to observe these guys. I started emulating what they did because I knew that was going to move me to my goal faster.

There was no way I could handle the giants at Waimea, but I spent a good deal of time watching the guys who could, studying their maneuvers, and promising myself I'd be back to ride those waves someday.

I stayed my three weeks, surfed the smaller waves, and did well in certain conditions. But I found that I was lacking the larger the surf got. I just didn't have the background. I was okay, I was comfortable, but there was a whole new canvas here. When you start going that fast and you're not accustomed to it, you've got a lot to learn. It was shocking to me how good the no-name local guys were. I knew I'd have a long way to go before I was anywhere near their league.

* * *

When I came back to California and started chasing down large waves and having a good time, my experience in Hawaii made me really comfortable in most situations. I was still living in the mountains and coming down to Santa Cruz and San Francisco seeking out larger waves, but they were rare. The average surf was only around waist-high. Plus, there were a lot of flat days and a lot of days that were too stormy and sloppy. When you factored all of that in, if I went on a surf trip and caught chest-high waves that day, I'd be pumped because I knew there were so many ways I could have gotten skunked.

CHAPTER NINETEEN

Four months after I got back from Hawaii, Diane found out she was pregnant. It was very exciting and we started envisioning our future together. She had been working in the casinos, and she left her job and found a gynecologist down in Berkeley. Our plan was that she would spend the last month of her pregnancy in Hayward with her mom to be close to her doctor. I'd keep working until it was time to have the baby because Tahoe and Berkeley were only about three hours apart.

After our son Josh was born, though, our relationship began falling apart. Because of the family dynamic as I saw it, my assumption was that Diane and I would remain married, but after two more years and several attempts at reconciliation, we both knew it wasn't going to work.

We were still trying to keep it together as a family when Lake Tahoe went through a building moratorium. Erosion was polluting the lake and causing the water to lose its pristine clarity, so the government agency in charge of the lake shut down all building. Well, if you're in construction that's a very clear statement.

The population had reached a tipping point. The first year we were in the mountains, there had been maybe fifty cars total in the parking lot at either Squaw Valley or Pine Meadows. That last year there were no fewer than 1500. I'd had an incredible time, and I had been so lucky to be there in those early days, but I could see the writing on the wall.

We found a house in Santa Cruz on the West Side, but I still needed to find work. So I grabbed a stack of dimes, went into a phone booth, and just started calling contractors out of the phone book. I had to take some non-union jobs for a while until I finally got a union gig up at U.C. Santa Cruz. Around that time, Diane moved out, and we split custody of Josh and broke up for good.

* * *

Shortly after I got back to town, I started surfing Steamer Lane again. There were these three high school kids who often surfed the Lane at the same time as me, and one afternoon one them called out, "There's Frosty!"

I've always had very blond, whitish hair that doesn't get dark when it gets wet, so it's an easy identifier out in the surf. I didn't think much of it at the time. Those kids hadn't been around before I moved up to Tahoe, so they had no way of knowing my name— to them *I* was the new guy. In surfing, a lot of people end up with nicknames because you need to be identified just for reference, and of course there are a lot of uncomplimentary ones out there. After a few weeks, other people started calling me Frosty, and I realized it was going to stick. I didn't mind, though, since there were a lot worse names they could've tagged me with.

Having the local kids tag me was a positive thing because I was working more on fitting in. It's not so much that I needed to be accepted, but I wasn't trying to piss anyone off, either. There was still that limited number of waves and nobody really wanted to share because if they were sharing they weren't getting enough waves for themselves. There was a lot of the old hustling, jockeying, and positioning going on, and some people were trying to be as intimidating and overly aggressive as ever.

It was still in the back of my mind to try and bring some of that communal mountain spirit of helpfulness and love of the sport to my old neighborhood. Before I could be friendly enough to be able to talk to people and give them advice, though, I had to fit in, and they had to figure out who I was.

I used the lessons I'd learned about body mechanics from skiing and the new data I'd picked up surfing much faster waves in Hawaii to become a better free-style and contest surfer. Before long, I got to the point of having enough experience and knowledge surfing-wise, and dealt with enough younger kids, that I knew a little encouragement went a long way. It's the simple act of saying, "You're not having the success that I know you're looking for, so you may want to try this."

It wasn't a big deal, it was just a casual thing.

When I started on the swim team and I knew nothing, it was a struggle. It was frustrating not to be good—everybody wants to be good. When I reached the point of being good, I just wanted to share with somebody how to lessen their struggle a little bit, to make it a little bit easier for them. I didn't want to remove the hardship of not being good, but I did want to add the encouragement of, "You will get through this, and you will be able to be better."

If people didn't pass along what they've learned, we would never progress.

One of the most common mistakes people make in many things is that they don't know what to do with their hands. In surfing, if you clench your fists—which a lot of people do—you create tension in your forearms, which then goes through to your biceps and triceps, which in turn tightens up your chest. Now you don't have the flexibility to be loose, fluid, and responsive. So sometimes all it took for me to help another surfer improve dramatically was for me to tell them, "Open up your hands."

This got me wondering. What would happen if I could actually coach somebody? How would I do it? I started gathering a lot of little data points, a lot of information. For instance, if you're standing up and your foot is twisted the wrong way it inhibits your ability to do things. From there I began to figure out that every body part has a neutral position where you have the greatest ability for full body utilization. And if you're not in that position, you inhibit your ability to move; you limit your flexibility and your strength.

Bob Pearson, meanwhile, had progressed to having his own surf team to represent his boards. He'd load four to six kids into his Ford van and take them to the contests. Well, by then I figured I had something to offer. I started traveling with Bob and we would give the kids tips and strategies on the way to the contests all over the coast. Then we'd review their performances and coach them on the way back.

These guys were stuck with us. They ranged in age from sixteen to eighteen, with maybe the occasional fifteen-year-old. There was a lot of strategy that we began to teach them about how to be the most successful that you can be in a contest. They were already good enough that Bob wanted to sponsor them and have them on his team, but they hadn't yet figured out what to do with their potential. Being a little older, Bob and I had both spent a few years apiece learning the following: *Potential doesn't mean much if you don't put in the mental and physical work that is required to fulfill it.*

So the very first thing we taught them was: *You need to understand who you are, what you do that's good, and then try to figure out how best to display your strongest maneuvers and skills.*

Of course, to do this, we first needed to teach them how to get into the best position and get them to catch a wave so that they could actually put this lesson into practice. That required what I came to call, "putting something in the bank." We went through the grinder with each one of the kids. I'd say, "Okay, Matt, what are your best moves?" He'd tell me three maneuvers he was stoked about, and I'd come back with, "Okay, we're gonna go to a break where those maneuvers are going to be very difficult to pull off."

Bob and I had to keep changing the game on them to make them sharp and resourceful. A common theme was that everybody thought they were a great tube rider; so we'd take them to a break and say, "There's no tubes here. Now what are you going to do?"

We were trying to get each kid to connect with their thinking process and push it forward to seeing what was real and viable in terms of what was actually going on. We were trying to get them connected to some sense of reality. Traveling from five to ten hours each way to those contests, there was plenty of time to lay out for them what could go on with something as unpredictable as surf.

The same holds true for any athletic endeavor. In surfing, the variable is the surf itself; you never know what it's going to do. But how do you know what your opponent will do in any sport, or what the specific conditions will be at the moment you have to perform?

We were trying to make the guys understand: *You have to be as informed as you can be about the situation ahead, but the only part of it you can actually control is yourself.*

Bob had a very talented team, and they became a lot better by being exposed to our lessons because we were successful in our own endeavors—Bob was one of the most successful contest surfers in the state. We taught them that the first thing you have to understand is that you need to be able to catch the minimum number of waves in a heat, plus one. Because once the judges miss one of your waves, and invariably they do, it's nice to have an extra one in the bank.

We'd seen guys go through heats, and, because of their free-surfing expertise, they never appreciated the fact that they only had fifteen minutes to catch three to six waves. They'd waste the whole fifteen minutes because, conceptually, time was just not part of their deal.

On the way back, they'd tell us, "Well, there weren't any good waves!"

"But we talked about that beforehand. You have to surf what's there."

"But it was all shit. It wasn't any good. You can't surf in stuff like that!"

We'd laugh and it was like, "Yeah, but there's a concept here. This is what makes it a contest. It doesn't matter how good you are—you can't advance if you catch no waves. If you're not surfing, you not going to advance."

That was the real difficulty in dealing with kids who were stars outside of the contests. You watched them surf good waves and you'd think, "My God, this kid is unbelievable." Then they went to a heat and they wouldn't catch a single wave because they weren't paying attention to the rules of the sport. They were just thinking about how good they were. They were just that disconnected.

That's why it can be such a challenge to work with kids—sometimes their perceptions are so off-base. What we as experienced athletes and coaches take for granted hasn't clicked for them yet. They don't get it. Even though you've talked about it, that doesn't mean it has registered.

But there was nothing like being embarrassed to make a young athlete reassess their approach. First off, they had to hear it from Bob and me on the way home. Then they'd get home and it was even worse: everybody knew they'd left for a contest and, when they came back, everybody would ask, "So how did you do?"

Then they'd have to explain, "Well, I didn't catch any waves."

That happens once and then it's never going to happen again. That's just how kids are. As a coach, you can't be frustrated by it. Amused, yes, but they have enough embarrassment all on their own and you don't need to add to it to get improved results.

You need to explain, "Yeah, there weren't any good waves. That's why you need to take the time to spot waves ahead of time or check in with Bob and me, because we've been on the beach collecting data for you for two hours before the heat."

Bob was very intense about putting together all the data. A lot of times, I could be somewhat footloose about it in my own contest surfing, and there was a cost to that. That's why Bob was a better contest surfer, because sometimes back then *I'd* go brain dead and just think, "I want good waves."

Bob was very disciplined, and I eventually trained myself to be very disciplined as well. If I wanted success in a contest I'd turn on that discipline, but I didn't always take contests very seriously. Surfing was always bigger than that to me.

Still, there were times when I'd take contests way too seriously. I'd rather not compete at all than to fall into that hole. We expressed that to the team as well.

After I started coaching with Bob, most of the local kids around Santa Cruz got to know who I was, and it was just a natural progression for me to offer them advice if it looked like they were struggling. If there was a good kid who conducted himself or herself respectfully in the water, then it was just natural for me to say, "Hey, would you like some help?"

CHAPTER TWENTY

Josh was four when I met Brenda. She was a teacher at his preschool, and the first time I saw her I fell in love. It was a gorgeous, late spring afternoon and I had gone over to pick up Josh. I remember throwing him up on my shoulder and walking across the lawn to my truck when the most stunning woman came out on the deck. Before she even said anything, I was dumbfounded.

She was wearing coveralls with her dark-red hair down past her shoulders and the sun behind her. I just looked at her and I was in love. There's no other way to explain it. When people say that, unless you've experienced it, you don't get it. And if it happens to you, you totally get it. We were just meant to be.

She smiled and said, "Oh, hi," and I was still trying to find a voice and be cool. Somehow I managed to squeak out some words that sounded reasonable and that didn't reflect how moved I was. As I carried Josh back to the truck, I was telling myself, "Okay, you've already been in love and married and that didn't work out. Nobody could be that great. You may as well do this, blow it out, and get it over with. Then get back to being who and what you are."

For Brenda's part, she told me later that she was looking at me and thinking, "Oh, my God, this guy is not the marrying kind and he's nothing but pure trouble. Just stay away."

When I got up the nerve to ask her out a few days later, she figured I at least had some money and could take her somewhere nice to eat, but she was still sure that she wouldn't end up getting involved with me. Needless to say it didn't work out that way for either one of us. For whatever reason, she was as blown away by me as I was by her.

Things quickly became serious. Brenda got double pneumonia within two weeks of our first date. She was living in a house with a bunch of girls and sleeping on the floor. We'd gone out once and had a few conversations, but I was already in love with her, and I knew she wasn't going to get better sleeping on the floor in a house full of young women running in and out all day and night.

Well, I had a house. So I just said, "Look, this is ridiculous. I'm not really home very much. I drop Josh off at school in the morning, go to work, and pick him up in the afternoon. If there's surf, I drop him off with a neighbor for an hour or so, then I come home and fix dinner. Since you're sick, why don't you just take my room until you're feeling better and I'll sleep in the living room. It's all cool."

After a grand total of six weeks together we started talking about getting married—and somewhere in those discussions I had to tell Brenda that I wasn't legally divorced from Diane yet. That went over like a lead balloon.

Once I got the papers signed and the divorce was a done deal, we went to the east coast of Maryland so I could meet her parents and ask for Brenda's hand in marriage.

They had a long, wide farm-style kitchen table with benches along the sides and a chair at either end. Brenda and I sat on the benches like kids with Mom and Dad on either end. Brenda's older brother and her two younger sisters were all gone, so it was just Mildred, Lester, and the two of us.

I did what I thought was right and proper and very formally asked Lester and Mildred for Brenda's hand. I had a whole speech I delivered. Lester just looked at me and said, "Excuse me, son, could you repeat that? I don't think I heard it." And Mildred, who never stopped talking, suddenly had nothing to say.

So now I had to repeat the whole thing. The first time around I'd stayed cool enough, but now I was a blushing, sweating mess. It was under-the-thumbscrews excruciating. It seemed to take forever.

"Eh," Lester said, "works for me."

He'd just wanted to see me squirm. I definitely squirmed.

We got married at their farmhouse and it took us nearly a month to drive back to California.

Brenda was born in Annapolis and raised there until her parents bought the farm on the Eastern Shore. She went to boarding schools and then Goddard College in Vermont. Like I said, she was a redhead, like my mom, with freckles all over, and if you put her in the sun she would burn. Some of Brenda's people were so white they were blue, but she still really loved the water.

Her mother's side of the family were water people from Smith Island in Chesapeake Bay, and they could trace their ancestry back to John Smith himself. Mildred's father was a boat builder who drew customers from all across the Bay. Brenda's heart and soul was in the water.

So she was very cool about me taking off to go surfing whenever I could fit it in with work, as long as I came home for dinner. Then some local parents—at their kids' urging—asked me to help form the Santa Cruz Surf League and start coaching the new Soquel High School surf team. That meant juggling the school team, Bob's team, work, Josh, and Brenda, and still finding time to catch waves myself. Brenda didn't mind—that was who she'd married. Even after our son Lake was born, she never flinched.

All of that was before Mavericks.

CHAPTER TWENTY-ONE

Around town I was known as a guy who had an interest in larger waves, but when I started hearing the rumors about this monster surf spot called Mavericks, I was skeptical at first. It was supposed to be a series of reef breaks a quarter to half a mile off the coast of Half Moon Bay that could generate waves anywhere from twenty-five to sixty feet tall. Having been back from the mountains for eleven years, if there was giant surf in my backyard, I figured I would've heard about it.

Out of nowhere people started asking me if I had surfed there, and I would tell them, "No, I haven't." Eventually, I began making inquiries to find out what the deal was. I had a board that was 9′6″and big enough to ride really large waves—certainly the largest waves that I had ever seen in California. It was more than enough board for anything between Santa Cruz and San Francisco, and I'd used it on several trips to Hawaii, surfing the larger waves at Sunset Beach. That was as much wave as I could envision at the time.

One of the people I asked about Mavericks was a guy named Mark Goin, a surfer recently out of high school who I'd hired to do cleanup and stock work on a construction job.

"Frosty, I know the boards that you have," he said. Since large-wave riding hadn't yet returned to the popularity of the early 1960s, anyone who did it was always checking out your equipment. "You could surf there, but I know you. Your board will work on smaller days but, knowing you, you would go out when it got larger anyway, and that's really not enough board."

Well, I respected Mark and his abilities. What he said was very disconcerting because 9´6˝ is a really big board.

All I could say was, "Wow."

To get a blank any bigger than 9´6˝ you had to get on a waiting list with Clark Foam, and they only blew those blanks once a year in October. They made a certain number of blanks that they knew they could sell, and they didn't make any extras. Prior to the discovery of Mavericks, all of those blanks went to Hawaii. As more and more people started finding Mavericks and Clark started getting orders for large-wave blanks from guys in Northern California, everyone started to get curious what was up with that spot.

But because legitimate, acknowledged, big wave riders had not been there yet and had not quantified its true worth, Mavericks was blown off.

I put in an order for a twelve-foot blank and a 10´8˝, and I had to wait nearly a year to get them.

*   *   *

My first time out at Mavericks was a misty, raining morning in October of 1988. I had a weather box set up in my bathroom because we had moved out to a house in a canyon in Aptos, and that was the only room where I could get reception. I checked the box for the latest buoy readings. The maritime shipping industry had buoys throughout the ocean to track Northern Pacific storm systems via satellite. I knew from my research that the storm systems I was interested in typically followed the jet stream and, the longer a system stayed in one place over the water and generated consistent wind speed, the larger the waves were and the more they focused in on one particular direction.

NOAA—the National Oceanic and Atmospheric Administration—made that information from the buoys available on the weather box. It would give wave heights, wave intervals, and wave direction. This was all critical information for deciding where to surf—if you knew how to read the data. And I had spent a lot of time figuring out how to read the data.

I knew that a storm was coming but that it wouldn't be particularly disruptive for us. We were right on the southern edge of it and no strong winds were forecast. As was my habit, I threw several boards into the back of my van to handle a variety of surf conditions, including my new twelve-foot board. With the drizzling rain, I knew it wasn't going to be a very productive work day, given the particular stage of the construction project I was working on, so I took off for Mavericks.

From talking to Mark, I knew where to park and where to walk out. As I was driving along the coast about twenty-five miles from Mavericks, I came around a curve and I could actually see it from that far away. Even at that distance, one look at all that whitewater cascading over the dark green, rocky surf told me that the waves were truly significant.

The first thing I did was to paddle out and sit in the channel to watch. *Your first time in any new situation, you want to observe and fill in all the information you don't have.* By now I had heard a lot of stuff about Mavericks, but I didn't want to formulate my opinion based on other people's interpretation of what goes on. I wanted to put together my own data.

Sitting in the channel, I watched Jeff Clark paddle out. From what I had heard, Jeff had re-discovered Mavericks as a kid, and he'd had a hard time getting anybody to come check it out. Alex Matienzo, Jim Thompson, and Dick Knottmeyer had surfed the smaller breaks back in 1961, but they thought the bigger ones couldn't be surfed. So they named it Mavericks Point after Alex's German Shepherd "Maverick." Dave Dyk and Bill Watson had surfed the small breaks during that early period as well but, after that, no one was known to have tackled the monsters until Jeff did it in 1975. It stayed that way for years. In the first place, people couldn't believe it was there. In the second place, it took a minimum of twenty-five minutes to paddle out to the waves.

I saw one in the twenty- to twenty-five-foot range approaching. It moved a little differently, and its shape was very pleasing. It was a well-shaped, well-formed wave with a deep, beautiful curve developing. Because of the overcast and drizzle, it wasn't wind-blown. The weather was what we call heavy air.

I saw Jeff start to paddle and he was paddling harder and faster than anyone I'd ever seen. As he started his paddling, the bottom of the wave slope had not touched him yet. A few seconds later, the bottom of the slope touched him, and he went backward. He kept paddling at this furious pace, so intent and so focused, and I could not fathom how he went backward up the face of a wave.

I thought my eyes must have gotten it wrong. I just didn't know what to make of it because I had never seen anything like that before. Jeff caught and rode the wave, paddled back and caught another, and sure enough he went backward again.

I thought, "Wow, this doesn't compute. I've seen it twice and I still don't understand how it happens. I've been to Hawaii, I've surfed Sunset, and I've seen Waimea, and this is still totally new to me."

My heart started pounding in a rush of excitement and fear—this was obviously a totally legit huge wave and it was where

I lived! The whole world had suddenly changed. At the same time, I had to focus and put aside my emotions. It didn't matter how awesome it was to have these waves in my backyard if I couldn't ride them. So rather than get caught up in the thrill of the discovery, I started watching and turned it into an analytical process. There was only one question on my mind: *How do I ride this wave?*

Calm and focused, I could see that the wave was ride-able. But that backwards action was definitely something to pay a lot of attention to. It demonstrated the sheer power of the wave. It said, "This wave will kill you if you play with it."

That, too, was not emotional—certainly not to the wave. Every wave is a force of nature, but I could see right away that Mavericks had a hell of lot more force than almost any wave I'd ever witnessed.

And this was one of Mavericks' smaller days.

I left the channel and paddled to the takeoff area. My intent was to be very cautious on the first run. I wanted to try to figure out the first wave and all the little nuances you have to be aware of. They had flat spots in them, and I needed to set that flat spot up so that I could transition through it with speed. Some places get really intense and they have little racetracks on them where you have to go really fast. You have to pick a proper line in order to make it through that section. There's a lot of information that you have to gather.

When you're looking from the shore you tell yourself, "Okay, I think I got it." But that's nothing like riding the wave and being able to figure it out.

The wave at Mavericks has such significant energy that it doesn't look like any other wave. So I was seeing all of this volume, all of this tremendous wave face that takes so much longer to drop down than any other wave I'd ever experienced. The waves even sounded different. They cracked when they broke.

As I watched the bizarre way the water moved, I realized that the waves were actually sucking water below sea level. The wave had so much energy that it was pulling the front part of the wave lower than sea level as it was drawing water up its face. This created a trough at the bottom of the wave. It's only a foot below sea level, but you'd know when you were in it. Boards aren't designed to go uphill. They're great at horizontal and down, but no one ever planned for up.

I caught my first Mavs wave and was riding along, got to the inside and stuck my hand in the wave to feel what was happening. So I was picking up information visually, through my hand, and through my feet when suddenly the whole dynamic of the wave changed. The intensity of the water coming up the face accelerated like an avalanche in the wrong direction. I knew it was time to kick out.

When I kicked out, I felt that backward pull of the wave trying to suck me back into its face. It had some pop to it, which was very rare for California, whereas in Hawaii it happens a lot. After I rode it out, I had some data and I knew I could start to open up my surfing a little bit.

That's when the emotions kicked in. My skin tingled everywhere. Paddling back out, I could still feel the rushing sensation of the long, long moments of acceleration as I'd rode down the face of the wave. This was a world-class wave, and looking out over the water, I could see that more and more of them were coming.

With big wave surfing there's usually not a lot of waves to be had. That's one of the things that made Mavericks unique, especially in the early days. We were on the southern edge of a lot of sizeable North Pacific storms, so there were a lot of waves to be ridden and a lot of days to ride them. They were mostly twenty-five to thirty-foot faces—that's a lot of wave face for discovering how to ride so much power.

Anyway, I finished my day, stopped by the job site and got in a little work, then I went home. I had a lot to think about, and I was very pleased.

As I came through the door, Brenda said, "Hey, how did it go today?"

"It was fine."

"What did you do?"

"Just the normal," I said. "Went to work. Surfed."

She asked, "Anything else you want to tell me?"

"Nope."

She started in with the interrogation again. I didn't know what was going on. It wasn't normal for her to ask so many questions. But she put me through the wringer again and I said, "What's up? I told you what I did."

She just smirked at me and said, "Well, big boy, you might want to listen to what's on the answering machine."

It was full.

It turned out there had been a filmmaker named Steve Ambriel out on the water in a Zodiac inflatable. I thought he was just out watching; I hadn't really paid him much attention. What had happened was that he'd filmed Jeff Clark, Mark Goin, and me surfing Mavs and had taken the footage to Jeff's place, and showed it while I was still at work. Then Steve came into Santa Cruz and showed it to some people who knew me. Then they started calling the house.

They wanted to talk about it and congratulate me. Well, I hadn't prepped Brenda for any of that because I didn't even know it was happening. So I listened to a few of the messages and it was just, *Oh, shit! Busted!*

Brenda wanted to know, "What is this place and what's it all about?"

"It's called Mavericks," I said. "It's a big wave spot and this was my first day there. I don't know much more. I'm still processing, trying to figure it out. It's not like anything I've ever seen or surfed before."

Someone called and said Steve was going to show the video again that night. Usually once I was home from work I was in for the evening because that was family time, but Brenda told me to go ahead.

The video was very impressive and it gave me more data to process. Having watched the tape, I felt even more comfortable that Mavs was something worth paying attention to and trying to figure out. Knowing what the data was for that day, I had to wonder what Mavericks could expand to, because although the swell had been notable, we had much more significant, larger systems that came through during the season. The question was, "How big can it really get?" And: "How big can I really play?"

*   *   *

I became consumed with surfing Mavericks. The whole setup made it intriguing. If I was looking at it from the left it was one of the ugliest waves because it was doing things that you just don't want to see. It pitches forward and sideways at the same time to make a barrel. And all of that time it's doing things water shouldn't do—moving in two directions at the same time. I didn't even want to know how that was possible.

To paddle out from the north end, I had to be able to make the first 100-yard section in a really short amount of time so that my leash didn't get hung up on the palm kelp or the little jags in the reef. It was an interesting dance to do.

I'd wanted to surf the largest waves for a long time, and I no longer had to deny that part of me because it was suddenly right there in my backyard. I didn't need to travel hours and hours by plane to get to it. I never imagined that was going to be possible.

I was getting the bills paid, and every night was still family time. I could do all that and still surf large waves. I couldn't believe how lucky I was.

Unfortunately, I over-indulged. After that first season, anytime that Mavericks was potentially there, I dropped whatever I was doing and went because I was trying to fulfill a learning curve and there was a lot that I needed to know.

And I was going to learn the hard way.

*   *   *

One morning in the early days when I was still trying to figure out Mavs, I watched the water as usual to find out what the interval was between waves, how many were in a set, and how intense they were. It was important to get a visual because a lot of the buoys my data came from were twelve to twenty-four hours away. You never knew until you got to a surf spot whether the data was correct, if the waves were more intense than had been indicated, or if the waves were crappy because the local wind was interfering.

What I didn't realize was, I really wasn't paying enough attention, not at the level that Mavericks demands. I was more casually observing—the way I would with normal waves.

Steve Ambriel was out in the Zodiac again with his driver. I liked to catch a wave early in the set, let other people catch their waves while I was paddling back out, and then catch one of the end waves in the same set. So I caught one with about a twenty-five-foot face early in the set and I fell. I was fairly far inside. The accepted thinking of the day— formed in Hawaii—was that you could swim down below the wave and you would barely feel it as it slipped by above you and let you swim back up, which is the first thing I tried to do.

Here was the problem: We used wet suits—and those are flo-
tation devices. Plus, the way Mavs waves are shaped and how they
move, their energy goes way deeper than a normal wave. So I swam
down as far as my leash and my suit would allow, which was in
the neighborhood of fifteen feet from the board to my ankles. But
when the wave was going over me, I wasn't below its energy level
and instead of being able to swim under and up, I got grabbed by
the wave force, which proceeded to thrash the hell out of me while
it held me down.

Starting to run out of breath in the blackness, I thought: This
is what I'm *supposed* to do. This is what works in Hawaii. This
sucks!

When I came back up, another wave was right on top of me,
so I swam back down and took another underwater thrashing. I
tried that a couple more times before I realized that I couldn't keep
it up much longer. I didn't know how many waves there were in
the set, but I knew I was going into oxygen debt.

One of the unique things about Mavericks is that you can
get beat, but you won't necessarily get pushed under—sometimes
the whitewater will just roll you viciously along the top of the
water until its energy passes you by. Since I was getting beat and
thrashed anyway, I decided I might as well lie on the surface, curl
into a ball when a wave approached, grab a great big breath of air,
and take my beating up there. I started counting waves to keep my
little pea brain occupied. At the tenth wave I had already decided
this was ridiculous. I counted nineteen in all before it was over
with. What kind of wave comes in a set of nineteen? None that I'd
ever been on, that's for sure.

All through this ordeal, I could see Steve and his driver in the
Zodiac maybe seventy-five yards away and I could not make any
progress toward them—I just kept getting beaten back and rolled.
I knew that if they thought it was safe they would come on in and

A photo of my parents (Jacqueline and Loren) on their wedding day. They were married in Santa Cruz.

Josh and me in Santa Cruz. Dianne and I were no longer together.

Brenda and me in our house in Aptos. We were married, without kids yet.

Lake and Brenda at the canyon house.

Me, Lake, and Roque at the hospital.

Lake and Roque, who is about eight months old.

All of us after I paddled across Monterey Bay the first time. This was taken at the wharf near the beach in Monterey.

Zeuf and me on the day of our wedding in Maui, 2000. Our ceremony took place on the beach and was a gathering of friends and family.

Zeuf, me, Lake, and Roque at the beach.

Zeuf surfing in a contest.

Here I am longboarding at Scorpion Bay.

My gift to Jay of a gold-painted toy wheelbarrow was an inside joke among the surfing community.

Photographer Bob Barbour (right) hands Jay a print of the iconic shot of him at Mavericks.

Zeuf was told she had cancer again and would need chemo. Mike Gerhardt and I shaved our heads in support. This is me at Jay's memorial paddle out.

A photo of me a couple of years ago on one of my surfing adventures. I met so many great people, saw landscapes that were otherworldly, ate some incredible food, and indulged in many, many waves. I try to travel several times a year and give many gifts for all that I receive.

throw me a line. That wasn't happening. I was stuck and I wasn't moving until Mavericks got done playing with me. I was her toy.

Only when the set was over could I paddle back to shore and recover. There was nothing Steve could have done. The message could not have been clearer: At Mavericks, the only person who can save you is yourself.

* * *

I kept getting deeper and deeper, pushing the limits more and more. During that second season, our son Lake was just over a year old and we were about to have his second Christmas. Josh had turned ten the year before and had decided he wanted to live fulltime with his mother and grandmother, so it was just the three of us.

Brenda had a tradition that, until the morning of the 25th, you would never know Christmas was coming by looking at our house. There was no tree, no decorations, and no presents. But after Lake went to bed on Christmas Eve, Brenda took the tree, the lights, the ornaments, and the presents from where she had them stashed. Then she stayed up all night and decked the place out to the nines.

In the morning, I woke up and the house was transformed. It was just spectacular. When we were a couple, it was something to see, but now that she was a mom, Brenda took it to another level. I walked into the living room and was blown away. The amazement on Lake's face when he saw the tree and the lights strewn all over the living room—I don't have the words. The fire was going in the fireplace; the tree was six feet tall and sparkling with tinsel and Brenda's family ornaments. Lake's eyes just lit up. He was pumped.

Meanwhile, I had been anticipating a Christmas swell, and sure enough it was on the weather box. So I hung out while Lake opened his presents and then we sat down to breakfast. That was probably at about nine.

Then I told Brenda, "Okay, I'm gonna go surf Mavs. I'll be back later."

She was livid.

"I don't think so," she said. "This is Christmas."

"Well, Mavericks is on and I'm going."

The way Brenda was raised, you cooked on Saturday because Sunday was the Lord's Day and there were so many things you just did not do on that day. You could read a book, but you couldn't watch TV or work. You put on your Sunday best for church—I'm talking men in wingtips and full suit and tie, ladies in fancy hats and high heels with stockings. After that, you sat out on the porch and talked story with the family. Mildred and Lester had a Cadillac that they only drove to church. Holidays were similar—only a much bigger deal.

So I went into the doghouse big time. Brenda was beside herself that I would even consider doing what I was going to do.

I was just like, "Nope, it's on. I gotta go. I'll be back for dinner."

She wouldn't even look at me. She just turned and walked away.

Me, I had a great time. It being Christmas, there were only a couple of other people out. I went home, had dinner, and figured that the domestic storm had passed.

The next morning, we woke up and Brenda said, "All right, I'm laying down the law: you cannot have from late September until May to go play this Mavericks surf thing anytime you want. Because I am not going to have my life on hold while you do all of this. So you need to start getting your stuff better organized."

"But, babe," I said, "waves happen when waves happen."

"Don't *but babe* me!" she snapped. "You're smart enough, you figure it out. Because I'm telling you, it's unacceptable. You did it, I'm upset, and it won't happen again. *Carte blanche* isn't happening. You're going to be a very, very disappointed man if you think that's going on."

Well, what could I do? I listened. Like Brenda said, I had to figure out something, because Mavericks was way too big to give up. I had to pay attention to the storm systems and swells and start choosing my days more wisely. Every go-out was meaningful. They all gave me a lot to think about and put together. My surfing continued to improve because of all of that.

PART V
JAY

CHAPTER TWENTY-TWO

I was parked in my van at Pleasure Point overlooking the surf one afternoon when this skinny, curly-haired kid just strolled up and knocked on my window.

"Are you Frosty?" he asked.

"Yes?"

"I'm Jay Moriarity," he said. "I heard you coach surfing."

By then, I was coaching the high school team, Bob's team, plus I had put together a group of guys who wanted coaching independent of Bob because he wasn't always available when we weren't traveling to contests. But this kid didn't look old enough to be in any of those groups. He couldn't have been more than twelve.

Just out of curiosity, I asked him, "Where did you hear that?"

"You coach Kevin Miske. He's my woodshop teacher."

Kevin was one of the guys in my new group, along with Wingnut Weaver and Matt Tanner. They were all up-and-coming long board competitors, and they were all in their mid-twenties. While it was true that people around town knew I coached surfing, I was also known as something of a curmudgeon who wasn't entirely enamored with people. I had a family to spend time with, a job to do to support them, three groups of young people I was trying to coach, and waves of my own to catch in the mix—I didn't have a lot of time or patience for small talk and pleasantries. When I was surfing, I was in surf mode—trying to maximize the number of waves I could get, trying to improve and enjoy what I was doing.

So approaching me was a big leap of faith on Jay's part because people perceived me as irritable and hard to get along with. He had no way of knowing that I wouldn't just tell him to run along. Jay was risking a lot because he was afraid of being turned down. I have no problem opening the door for certain people, but I didn't want them to be presumptuous and assume that I'd coach anyone who asked me. But if they're carrying on the aloha spirit, laughing and having a good time, then sure thing.

I'd seen Jay in the water and he always had this wonderful grin on his face. He seemed like a good kid. Besides, he wasn't old enough to be a surf jerk.

So I said, "Kevin's a great guy. What can I do for you?"

He told me that Kevin had been giving lessons to him and some of the other kids from his class. Jay figured that if I was teaching Kevin he might as well jumpstart the process and come work with me directly.

"How old are you?" I asked.

"Twelve."

"Okay. What are you looking to do?"

That's when I was struck—like everyone else who ever met Jay—by the sparkle of his brilliant blue eyes.

"I want to be a better surfer," he told me.

From there I knew he was worth at least some of my time. Because the first piece was already in place. He saw himself as a surfer—that picture was in his head.

He had a vision.

He was starting off with a picture in his mind of what he wanted to accomplish. It wasn't well-defined yet—but as I've said earlier, it didn't really have to be.

You start off with something as simple as, "I want to be a surfer," or "I want to be a volleyball player." That vision of where you want to go and what you want to be, however vague, is how you begin the process.

Still, I remember thinking: This kid's twelve. Whatever you tell him, he'll remember it for maybe forty-five seconds before a girl walks by and he forgets all about it. But I figured if I gave him some basic pointers it would at least make him feel good that somebody had heard him out, so I was like, "Okay, cool."

Then I gave him the basics:

"To begin to be a successful surfer you have to be in condition. Practice your swimming and your paddling to get better at the process of being able to catch waves in the first place. When you get bored of being in the water, push-ups, sit-ups, and going for bike rides are all great alternatives; you need something else to do to get a different perspective. Those are the things I did," I told him. "And those are things I'd pass on to anyone who's interested in becoming a better surfer."

He thanked me and said he'd work on it.

Like I said, I never really thought it would go anywhere. Most people don't understand the work it takes to become good at anything. I expected Jay to have a twelve-year-old's attention span, so I didn't expect a whole lot. But six weeks later I was still seeing him working on his paddling and riding his bike, and I thought, The little shit took it seriously!

I didn't know yet how deep Jay's passion went, but it was totally cool to see him doing the work. I wondered if he would actually come back and follow up with me or if he was going to take off on his own. Kids can be very independent, and they also look to their peers for a lot of background information on how to do things. I didn't want to see that happen. It's something I mentioned earlier. What I remembered from being on the high school swim team, and trying to figure out why everyone got cold when I started to lap them, was that going to your peers for advice was only slightly better than trying to figure things out on your own. *At best, your peers are only equal to or a little ahead of you, so they're not ideal teachers.*

Fortunately, Jay came back to me and said, "Okay, Frosty, I've been doing the work."

"Yeah, I've seen you," I said. "You've been doing good. Now let's go ahead with trying to figure out how to get you better at catching waves."

That meant getting in the water with him.

With Jay being such a beginner, he hadn't had enough experience to collect a decent amount of meaningful data that he could refer back to and work from. Until he had that data, it would be hard to develop a dialogue with him to help him start evolving toward where he wanted to be. The method I'd been using was to ask people what they wanted to achieve and then get them to realize that, to reach that level, they had to break it down into smaller, more attainable steps. That had become my process.

With the older kids, I would start off by assigning them essays. Because surfing is a dance linking certain specific maneuvers together with as much grace and fluidity as possible, I would ask my students to list all of their maneuvers and give me a percentage of successful completions for each of them. I had them write out breakdowns of the moves they wished they could do, what they were already decent at, and what they had mastered. Then I'd move on to a discussion of their best wave, their worst wave, their best experience in the water, those sorts of things.

But because Jay was so young, he didn't have that level of experience to draw from. Plus, I had to be careful about how I would bring him along; I didn't want to overwhelm him or turn him off.

I wanted to do things that were going to keep him interested and excited. So we started to surf together.

The neighborhood kids got into surfing with whatever they could get their hands on—garage sale boards and giveaways mostly. Some of those boards had been passed down in Santa Cruz for generations. Jay had a pretty decent old long board that he'd borrowed from his mother's boyfriend.

"We need to get into the water," I said. "And then what do we do?"

"Well, then we go surfing?"

"Okay, but when we get in the water, what do we do?"

"We get in the water and … I don't know."

That was pretty much what I figured. Most people start surfing without ever knowing the very basics.

"For everything that you do," I said, "you need to develop a plan. You need to visualize what's going to happen. So, yeah, we're gonna get in the water, but before we do, we need to know what's happening with the swell. For that, we have to listen to the weather box. Certainly, you can see what's happening straight out in front of you, but you also need to understand what the ocean is doing. If you listen to the weather box several times a day, you'll be able to figure out if the swell is coming up or if it's going down."

I stopped to see if he was taking any of it in. From the look in his eyes, he was.

"You need to know that, because the other thing you need to understand is what's happening with the tides, which is the ocean depth rising and dropping, possibly in conjunction with a large incoming swell. If you're going to go out, you need to plan how long you can stay out. So what's the next thing that happens?"

Jay flashed me that smile. "*Then* we surf?"

CHAPTER TWENTY-THREE

Jay and I surfed Pleasure Point because that was a fun, playful break near his house, but it still had its challenges.

"You should get yourself a weather box," I told him. "You can pick one up for less than ten bucks, and if you listen to it then you'll know when the swell is going to get bigger and when the tide is going to come up. You need to know that, because there are plenty of broken legs around here already."

I was referring to all the people throughout the winter season who ended up injuring themslves in the rubble, the large blocks of rock and concrete set up along the cliff to protect it from wave erosion. That loose, haphazard placement of material is slippery and incredibly awkward to negotiate even on a day when you don't have waves breaking over you.

And I was trying to get Jay to understand the bigger picture: While we were doing something he was already doing all the time, there could be bigger consequences than he might be prepared for. He got it almost instantaneously. For a lot of people—I don't know why—I'm hard to understand. But that wasn't the case with Jay. We were on the same wavelength from the very beginning, so his assimilation was very quick.

Once we were in the water, I watched him so that I could get an idea of what he was doing, why he was doing it, and how he linked his different maneuvers together. A lot of our initial work was based around position in the water and wave data. What makes surfing so difficult is that, unlike when you're skiing—a body in motion on a mountain—both you *and the mountain* are moving. So not only do you have to master the physical aspect of it, but you have to be able to look at waves and see what they're doing, where they're going, and where you want to be on them. On top of that, you have to understand the intensity, strength, and size of the waves. It's facilitated a lot by being at the beach, watching people and referencing what they're doing, and discussing how there might be a different interpretation of that rhythm or dance.

We started working on just being able to stand up and link moves. From there we got into riding and reading waves. Riding waves is all about learning to be in the right place, doing the right maneuver, at the right time. So the first thing he needed to know was how to get to the right place.

Most beginner surfers have no clue how to do that—they don't know how to establish where the waves break. They need to learn to watch the waves break from the beach, go to that spot in the water, and then use a technique called triangulation so that they can find it again.

I led Jay out to where the waves were breaking that day and explained, "You are one point of a triangle. Now the idea is to establish the two other points. For each point, pick out something on the shore that you can easily see from here, and then pick another one behind it to establish a straight line in that direction."

Jay chose a telephone pole and a corner of the building behind it.

"Okay, now swing around a little in the other direction—anything from thirty to ninety degrees—and pick out two more points to establish the second straight line."

Jay set up his second line and saw what it meant right off: Once he'd found the right spot to catch waves on any given day, he could find it again and again on his own.

"Are you kidding me?" he laughed. "It's that simple?"

"You can see for yourself," I said. "But some people don't learn it for years."

In fact, surf instructors are notorious for paddling out with someone, showing them where to catch a wave, and then abandoning them while they surf the wave themselves. They're not giving their students even the most basic building block—where to find the break—so now you have someone floating around out in the ocean without a clue what to do about it, no idea of what's expected of them, or how even to begin to be successful at this process of surfing.

Jay caught on quick, but that's not to say he was particularly good at first. When you paddle into a wave, you're looking at what's going on, and you're either successful or you're not in whatever it is you're attempting to do. If you're not successful, you need to be able to relate what happened back to your coach. So Jay would relate back to me, and we would discuss why something he was trying didn't work. I don't coach from a critiquing perspective; I'll never tell someone what they're doing is wrong. I'll simply ask if that's what they really *want* to be doing. If you are given the chance to explore alternatives, then you can say, "Okay, these are the changes I want to make." Because you're actually thinking about what happened and why it happened.

Like any other surfer, Jay would fall, he'd paddle after waves just to have them slip out from under him, and he'd get distracted by some nonsense and blow a maneuver that should've come easy.

The difference with Jay was that none of that ever wiped the smile off his face.

He already knew what all the great skiers on the mountain knew, and what the aggressive, territorial surfers never understand: *You're supposed to be having fun.*

Having fun is a fundamental that young athletes rarely learn because so many coaches and parents don't know it either.

In the water, we would see some very poor excuses for people performing as athletes, slapping the water and cursing and having their little temper tantrums. And they think that's acceptable. They're not aware of what that kind of behavior creates in your body. We're an electrical circuit: If your body is happy, energy flows better through it. When you start feeling angry and tense up your muscles, you end up just a hiccup behind because of all that unnecessary stress.

The best athlete on the court, on the field, or in the water is the person who's having the most fun. You're going to fail sometimes, everybody does. As a surfer, I fall off my board all the time—I'm trying things. A lot of people say, "Oh, he's not very good. Look at him, he falls." Well, we all learn more by falling than by succeeding. So, stop learning and you won't fall anymore. But if you want to keep growing, you have to keep experimenting and falling down.

"You cannot get frustrated," I explained to Jay. "You see people having these little episodes. Look at what they're doing. Are they happy? Are they laughing? No. They're angry, they're hostile. If doing this makes you angry and hostile, you should be doing something else."

And I made sure to tell him again and again: "*If you're not falling down, you're not learning.*"

Of course I couldn't know that he was going to prove the truth of this in truly dramatic fashion.

CHAPTER TWENTY-FOUR

Jay was always the happiest guy in the water, though he sure wasn't always the best. In those early days, he looked as awkward as any beginner, but I admired all the work he'd been putting in to try and get better. He reminded me of myself, driving nail after nail into a chunk of wood until I could drive them straight because I wanted to become good at what I was trying to do.

Jay was the same way. His enthusiasm for wanting to become good meant that if I asked for ten push-ups, he would give me fifteen. If I asked for forty-five minutes on the bike, he'd give me an hour. The way he saw it, why cut it short? Why try to cheat? Why not give more? The two of us—and I think all successful people—are like that. *This is what I want, why would I shortcut it?*

It was only after he started putting in a lot of the work that Jay began to look different from the other kids in the neighborhood and develop a style of his own. By that time he was confident in being able to get up, do a bottom turn, get trim, and start doing cut-backs. And once he started learning about biomechanics, he was able to actually leverage the board and start pulling off more advanced maneuvers. Through it all, he was still having a good time . . . most of the time.

As much as Jay impressed me, he was still a normal twelve year old in that he could be skittish and uncertain. At times he was very unsure and uncomfortable about how to be and who to be.

The surfing community in Santa Cruz was like growing up in Hayward—everybody knew everybody else's business. And everyone knew that Jay's mom, Christy, had a drinking problem. His dad wasn't in the picture because he was in the military, stationed in Panama, and Christy would act out in public. Jay never wanted me to pick him up at home, and I knew from experience what that was all about.

For the first few months that we were getting to know each other, we never spoke about it. I didn't want to embarrass him, and I didn't want to interfere with or substitute for his parents but as we spent more time together it was hard for me to just watch his frustration and not say anything. Finally he showed up at the beach one day after school and he was particularly distracted. Something had happened with his mother, but he wouldn't tell me more than that.

I wasn't about to address Christy's issues. So before we paddled out, I spoke to him about his family situation as being just the way life is—that he would face lots of challenges and had to start learning how to successfully get through them.

"You have to understand that your mom and dad are trying to do the best they can for you and for themselves," I said. "Sometimes it just doesn't work out. I've been married before and it didn't work out. I'm not going to fault my ex completely and I'm not going to fault myself completely. The basic component of people is that they want to do the best they can, but the best that they can possibly do, you know, sometimes it falls short. That's very hard, but that's very real."

Jay just nodded and muttered, "I guess."

"I know your dad loves you," I added, "but he's moving around, and your mom, she's not moving around. I don't know what separated them, I don't know what their differences are, but I don't need to know. My interest is you. But keep in mind that you never know where anybody comes from or who they are and all of the stuff they had to go through to become who they are."

"I hear you," he said and started heading for the water.

We got in a couple hours of surfing. Jay's maneuvers got cleaner and more fluid, as usual. Also as usual, by the time we were done for the day, Jay had made a bunch of new friends.

Back on the beach, I told him, "You are unique. You have this incredibly disarming smile and those blue eyes. And there's a bunch of hard-ass guys out there, but you have the ability to paddle up to them and go, 'Hey guys, how're you doing? What's up?' Nobody does that, not the way that you do it."

There was that smile again.

*   *   *

Before long, Jay was good enough to surf Steamer Lane. It was a hot, crowded day and I pointed out all the older kids lined up in the pit.

"It's very rude to just slide into a surf break and take waves ahead of the people who were there before you," I said. "It's usually first come, first served, deepest in the pit gets the wave. You need to honor that. If the people ahead of you aren't interested in a wave, you can take it, but when you paddle back out you're in the back of the line again. The person who's sitting out the furthest and the deepest is looking for special waves, and that's a big investment of time, so it's *really* rude to paddle around them and take off.

"All you need to do is what comes naturally," I continued. "You're very courteous and very respectful. Be that person. I've got your back. Nobody's going to give you shit and if they do I'll intervene and try to defuse the situation. Once they see that you can surf, it will be cool. A lot of times you'll go into an area where people don't know you and it'll take a while to get them to warm up to you because each new person means there's less waves for everyone else. It's important to let the locals have their waves."

And of course Jay just took off and started adding new members to his fan club. He didn't seem to notice or care if someone looked like a hard guy or started puffing up his chest. He'd watch someone and just beam at them, shouting, "Awesome wave, dude!" and "Nice one!"

People I wouldn't think to talk to were paddling over and high-fiving him after he caught a nice wave. Then he'd fall off, get totally beat, and just come up laughing. Just watching him was infectious. Everyone laughed along with him.

*   *   *

As I worked with Jay, he moved through the maturation process much faster than most people—certainly much faster than I had. He just got it. He picked up on one thing and asked for more. It was exciting for me to be around someone who was proving to be such a really special person. It was going to be interesting to see as he got older. Even though he was going to be home-schooled instead of having the usual high school experience, there were still going to be a lot of potential distractions. He was going to have a lot of challenges figuring out what he was supposed to be doing, and I just wondered where surfing would fit in with all that.

I was working with him on so many different levels, and the personal level was just starting to evolve. Our relationship was deepening because Jay was becoming more capable of being involved. He was becoming an older, more mature human being.

We'd go to this great little restaurant called Cliff Café after a session, and I'd ask him, "How did you treat the waitress? Were you an unreasonable jerk who could not make up his mind and blamed her? Or did you see that the restaurant was packed and everything was falling behind? Did you say thanks to the cooks? Did you try to make someone's day better?"

These were rhetorical questions, of course, since Jay merely had to be present to make someone's day better. But I wanted him to acknowledge his own progress as he was learning to become not only an athlete, but a complete human being. That's why I started sharing stories with him. As he progressed, I became very aware that I was investing a lot in him personally, and I became very aware of the most important thing in sports:

It's easy to make a good athlete. It's very hard to make a good human being.

* * *

It was a warm, sunny day, not much wind, and Jay and I were on East Cliff Drive at Pleasure Point, leaning against the back of the van as we watched the waves coming in.

We were talking about what the waves were like—how consistent, the size, which boards to ride—when a car approached from the west and the people inside started waving at me, so I waved back.

Jay asked, "Who was that?"

"I have no idea," I said.

He just nodded and said, "Cool." It didn't occur to him to ask why I had waved back at people I didn't know.

CHAPTER TWENTY-FIVE

I had been working with Jay for about a year when he showed up at the beach one day and announced, "I want to be a contest surfer."

Right away I knew that everything up until then had been the easy part. Being a good surfer isn't simple, but it's natural in that there's only you, your board, the waves, and your ability. With contest surfing, there are rules and structure imposed on all of that. At thirteen, Jay was still younger than anyone I had trained to surf at contests. And even as an adult, I had found it difficult at times to impose contest discipline upon myself. Although Jay certainly had passion, it remained to be seen if he could handle things like strategy and discipline.

Still, he had earned the right to take it to that next level if he could.

I asked myself, "What is the best way to do this? How can I make this happen the simplest way possible?"

I needed to establish a whole new set of reference points for Jay because, again, success is very difficult when you first attempt something new—you start off knowing nothing and, along the way, you have so much to learn that you forget where you began.

That's where writing lists and diaries came in. I told him, "You're going to start getting better, you will be taking on new maneuvers, and there's going to be a lack of success as you try out new things. So there's going to be a lot of frustration because, as you become good at one thing, you'll try something else, which means starting all over again. *Overall, you'll be progressing and it's important not to lose sight of that progression. The best way to do that is to keep track of your accomplishments.*

"So let's start with making some lists today. Write down where you are; list all of your maneuvers and your success rate for each one. And then, just for fun, list all of the maneuvers that you would want to do."

He just said, "Oh, okay."

It was the formalizing of a thought. A complicated task has many elements to it, so it's a process, and it's easy to get lost in the process and forget where you began.

For Jay, so much of the process was getting him to understand who he was and who he wanted to become.

Having a vision was the first step.

Now Jay had finally expressed that he had a dream.

Well, I believe in dreaming—and dreaming big. I've lived a life that was not what I had been told it would be. The life I had been told about in so many of the messages from my family, my friends, and the media had always sounded so boring to me. There was no adventure, no excitement, no reason for being here. People went to work at some mundane job all their lives, and at the end the boss didn't even give out the gold watches anymore. Some deal.

So I was definitely going to do whatever I could to help Jay achieve his dream. At the same time, though, reality was shouldering its way into my own life.

I had coached the high school team for six years. It was great, it was a blast, but Brenda and I had Lake, our daughter Roqué had been born, and I needed to start providing a more substantial and sustainable income. I could make mortgage payments most of the time without too much trouble and still be able to play, but sometimes I really had to put in a lot of effort to make sure I could cover those payments. Economic conditions being what they were, it became very difficult in the residential construction market to have the kind of financial security I wanted for my family. I had plenty of sleepless nights thinking about how I was going to be able to put the whole deal together.

It was putting a lot of strain on our relationship. I was off making commitments in the community, which is great as long as you can meet your commitments at home. Coaching Jay and coaching the older guys all fell into my own surf time—it happened when I was available, on my schedule. The high school team was necessarily more regimented, so I had to phase it out and make more time for working.

I had struggled and struggled until I had finally lined up a solid six months of work. Everything else was going to fall into place. Bob Pearson was getting ready to remodel his house, and I told him I could give him two weeks for whatever he needed. I ended up doing the demo phase, because Bob can be a procrastinator and needed to get the project started, so I just went over to his house one day and tore the roof off.

"By the way," I told him, "you're started."

After that, I went by my buddy Everett's job site on a commercial project. We had been foremen together, and he had been brought in as superintendent on this job because the guy who had been there before him had failed at getting it done on time and on budget. Everett said he wanted to bring me on as the foreman.

This project was so enticing because it was commercial, which meant it was much more reliable work. The job was going to take six months, so I was going to have a steady source of income.

Everett told me that the company we were working for treated its people really well. They promoted from within and liked to keep their people employed all the time. That was music to my ears. Brenda was going to be a lot happier, because we could build up the bank account and we'd have health insurance.

Meanwhile, Jay had written out his first assignment. After that, it was time for him to see for himself what contest surfing was all about.

"Okay, fine," I said. "You want to be a contest surfer? Let's go watch some contests. Let's see what other people do and where you fit into the process; that way, I can begin to show you what maneuvers you need to add to your list of things you can successfully complete. And from now on, every time you go surfing, you select three things from that list to focus on. Don't overwhelm yourself. Select two maneuvers from the list of things you can already do and that you're working on, plus one from your wishlist. It gives you a good focal point, and it's a nice way to keep your presentation fresh."

Where until now we had been meeting maybe once a month, we upped it to every week, practicing and watching competitions together.

At that point, it made sense to introduce Jay to Brenda and our kids because we started to spend more time together. I can't do anything halfway. If I go to do something and I commit to it, you're going to get all of me. That was becoming real apparent.

Jay was really easy to hang with. We had a lot of the same interests. It just worked, it fit, and having him around was cool. The house back in the canyon needed a lot of work, so I'd go over to Santa Cruz when there wasn't any surf, pick him up, and we'd work on the house together.

The first time I asked Brenda if it was okay to bring him over for dinner, she said, "Of course it is. I was wondering when you were going to ask."

From that day on, our family started to include him in the things we were doing. He'd often come over and hang out with Lake and Roqué and Brenda while we talked surf. I'd hurt my back on the job, so I would come home from work after surfing, lie on the floor, and the kids would come snuggle up in my arms, one on each side, while Jay sat over us and we discussed his progress. It was really obvious that it was a relationship that he cherished. He cultivated it. It became very evident that he was missing a balance of male and female energy in his life. He felt that the relationship between his mom and her boyfriend Stan was different. Christy and Stan were trying to figure out their deal, and there were challenges in that. We certainly were not replacing them, but it was never remotely conceivable that we would distance ourselves from Jay.

* * *

Before the first contest I took him to, I told him, "One of the things that I have learned, and that you need to learn, is that you need to be who you are, and you need to be who you are all the time. Watch these guys and see how they change. There's a lot of surf people who are your best friend on land. They'll sit down, talk story with you, laugh with you, tell jokes, and it's all good. Then you get in the water and they're going to burn you. They won't get your board if your leash breaks—they're just in it for themselves. You'll have the opportunity to see every type of personality in the water, and you will be able to choose whoever it is you're going to be. It's important to figure that out. Who do you want to be?"

As the contest got going, Jay saw surfers in way over their heads, people without much of a display, without serious maneuvers, who maybe didn't measure up to other people all that well. He got to see how taking off late and blowing it goes. The main thing I wanted him to see was the difference between the results you get from selecting a low quality wave compared to selecting a good one.

"Take that with you every time you get in the water," I said. "How choosing the right waves opens you up to being able to pull off so many more maneuvers. But remember," I added, "that's only for days when there are plenty of good waves. The first rule is always: Surf what's there." *Work with what you're being given.*

Of course, that was just the beginning.

The thing that makes surf contests such troublesome events is that there's so much strategy involved, and everything is built around understanding the rules. Most of the contests that Jay would be competing in were six-man, fifteen-minute heats, where you're judged from one to ten on your three highest scoring waves. The criteria the judges are looking at in each heat are the largest waves ridden for the longest distances, with the most radical maneuvers pulled off in the most critical part of the waves. The variable is how many sets of waves the ocean gives you in a certain time frame and how many waves come in a given set.

That's why it's so important in contest surfing for somebody to be gathering that data for you on the beach. Most young surfers aren't sponsored or even on a team, and they don't have parents who are knowledgeable enough to watch the waves and tell them what's going on. So that would be part of my job.

Athletes spend a lot of time watching other athletes, and hardly any time watching themselves. Something that seems easy, like seeing yourself perform a maneuver in the mirror, recognizing what isn't working, and then being able to make changes in that process, is actually very difficult for a lot of people. Neither one of us had the money to buy a video camera, so I had to teach Jay the visualization technique.

Initially, Jay was not a fan. It's not that he didn't grasp the concept. It was just that, like any thirteen-year-old, he didn't love the idea of slowing down. Writing essays and visualizing both required him to go off someplace by himself, be quiet, and just think hard. Sure, Jay was a deep thinker for a teenager, but at that age he wasn't crazy about being home, or being alone.

"It's what you need to do," I tried to explain. "Because you can be in the water doing what seems normal, natural, and familiar, but you can't think about what you're doing when you surf—you can only surf. If you get out, relax, and visualize what your body is supposed to be doing, then you do it in a mirror, and you'll realize, 'Oh, is *that* what I actually look like?' Allotting the time in your life to actually do that, on a daily basis, will help you improve."

For him it was a distraction from what he wanted to be doing. He was a guy and he wanted to be out doing guy things. But he also wanted to do what he knew would get him results, and that's where his frustration lay. I could tell by his tone of voice that there were times when he would rather being doing other things. Sometimes we'd be talking and he'd have a very flat affect. There were other things going on in his life. And the fact is, he would rather be surfing than talking about it. Being in the water was the most important thing to him.

I finally told him, "Look, Jay, you don't have to do what I'm telling you, you don't *have* to do anything. But I know what works."

"Okay, *okay!*" he laughed. Then he started doing it.

Most athletes, especially young athletes, never do. Which, again, is why it takes that initial passion, the desire, to reach your true potential.

CHAPTER TWENTY-SIX

Along with the mental work, there was a whole lot of physical work Jay still had to put in before I was going to take him to his first contest. While he had some strength, it wasn't consistently developed, and I didn't want him to become too strong without knowing the proper way to use his strength.

Strong surfers can learn how to overpower waves, but that doesn't make you a good surfer. A lot of athletes come up against other athletes who will try to out-muscle them, out-strength them. They're perceived as being the better athlete, but that's not necessarily the case. Somebody who has better technique will ultimately win out. If you continue to pursue technique, you will find a way to be better than people who are bigger and stronger than you.

Just as in basketball where they have big man footwork camps, in surfing people have to learn where their body is in space and how it does what you're trying to get it to do. You have to understand the biomechanics of doing a certain maneuver while at the same time setting yourself up to do the next maneuver and the one after that, so that you have this continuity of motion that creates a visual rhythm.

"You're very strong," I told Jay, "But you need to learn technique. Keep working on your biomechanics. Learn how to leverage your arms. To learn how to use your arms, first you learn how to use your fingers and hands, which sets up your elbows, which sets up your shoulders, which sets up your knees. Everything has to be in alignment. You can muscle through—or you can learn technique."

Another thing Jay needed to work on was his ability to look at a wave and know how fast he would have to paddle to be able to catch it. He was at the right age to be able to build his strength, so I upped his workout program of riding the bike to build up leg strength and lung capacity, as well as to build up the muscles in the arch of his back to be able to get the stroke down with some consistency so that, once he could read a wave, he'd be able to get to the right place at the right time.

As he began to get stronger and paddle faster, he still needed to learn how to look at a wave and know when to start paddling before his success rate at catching waves would go up. The idea is that the wave needs to reach a certain steepness and you need to put yourself and the surfboard in the spot where the wave is steep enough to catch, but not so steep that if you do catch it you don't have time to stand up before it breaks.

I told him, "Everyone wants to try to put their board perpendicular to the wave to try and catch it that way. What actually happens when you do it that way is that the board maximizes its speed very quickly and then goes to the bottom of the wave where it instantly slows down. But just turning your board and getting a little bit of an angle draws out the time, because you've now extended how long it takes between first catching the wave and getting to the bottom by creating a longer diagonal. So you've got more time to get up."

I taught him pop-up exercises where you get on the floor like you're doing a push-up but then pop up and get your feet underneath your body as fast as you can.

With all this work, Jay was improving rapidly. He was changing from an awkward beginner into an accomplished surfer. He was developing a style of grace and strength that was very technically correct.

None of that did him any good when he blew his first significant contest.

*   *   *

It was a ten-hour drive down the Pacific Coast Highway to Baja, a run I'd made many times with Bob and his team. This time, though, it was just Jay and me, and he was subjected to the usual treatment without anybody else around to deflect it. We took off Friday and drove all day, talking about how the contest was formatted, what he was thinking about doing, evaluating different wave conditions, and going through every possible scenario.

I especially drilled him on strategy—putting something in the bank.

"Some surfers spend a lot of time and energy trying to catch waves that are not going to advance their cause. A wave that you can score a four on is a medium-scoring wave. With a six you're starting to get to something special. But once you've got that score in, you want to up your average. Now, instead of looking for a five or six, you want a seven or eight. You can't leave a heat with just one good wave. You need two medium waves and one high-scoring wave, or two highs and one medium, all the while bearing in mind that, above all, you have to take what you can get.

"As you enter the water," I said, "you'll know what it's going to take to build your bank account. You can focus your time at the event toward very specific goals. Then you can cross things off the list. Like, 'Okay, I have one medium wave. Now I just need one high scoring wave and another medium.' You know you've got one set that will have a high-scoring wave potential in it, so you have to decide, do you take a really nice medium-looking wave, or do you wait it out for a big one?"

We'd already worked out a whole series of signals that I could give him from the beach to help him out with dilemmas like that. But if you don't have a spotter, you need to rely on the best information you've been able to gather for yourself. So before you enter the water, you want to evaluate where you need to be, how much time you want to invest in a particular area where waves may be breaking, and what may present itself as you're paddling back out. When sets are coming and everyone's in the process of getting into position, you need to figure out how to move into the best position among all these other players, each of whom wants exactly the same thing.

But since this wasn't a local contest, Jay had a third option.

"When we get to the beach, find out who the best local surfer in your heat is going to be and sit on them. Wherever they go, you go. Because they know all of the subtleties of the break, they'll be able to pick the best waves in a set and save you a lot of time having to figure that out. Watch where they go to take off on a wave when everyone's setting up."

"Okay, cool," Jay said.

"But after that," I warned him, "don't watch their maneuvers. Don't even look at them."

Jay nodded. Then did exactly what I told him not to do.

Good waves had been predicted, but the weather system fell apart during the drive down. The waves were only waist-high and rather weak. Being a bigger guy, I always prefer at least chest-high, but Jay was still a kid so it really shouldn't have made any difference for him. He was small, but he had strength and grace. If the waves were larger, they would have played to his strength factor. Still, we had talked about this—you had to surf what was there. He didn't waste the whole heat waiting for a perfect wave like a lot of the older guys I'd coached, he went for what there was to get, but his head just wasn't in it.

It's not that he wasn't already very capable of performing. He was just so much like I'd been—young, numb, and dumb.

Once the contest got going, I could see him losing his focus. That's not unusual; when you're in the water and you're looking back seeing people who are watching you, it can be very unsettling. But as a competitor you have to realize that you're stepping into an arena and that you are on display. The real problem is when instead you start to focus on the other surfers in your heat, and that's what happened with Jay. I wasn't so much watching him surf as I was watching him watch everyone else.

Meanwhile, no matter how I tried to signal him, Jay didn't seem to notice. Everything about his body movement told me that he'd been shaken up by watching the other contestants.

It's so easy to watch another surfer in your heat and say, "Wow, that guy's doing really good." Well, usually you're not at the end of where the surfer's going to finish his ride, or if you are, you probably didn't see the beginning. So you're getting a relatively small perspective of what is going on, and it absolutely has nothing to do with your job, which is to maximize what *you* can do. It's a distraction to watch what somebody else is doing and let it get under your skin, like, "Well, now I've got to get better because I just saw what that guy did."

Typically, you're only seeing three or four seconds of somebody's ride. You're all wrapped up in watching them and it's in your head now—you're trying to figure out how you're going to go ahead and put up maneuvers that are better than theirs, when your competitor might have fallen off right behind you. Or when you see a ride you thought was an eight or a nine was actually only a three because the kickoff was horrible and the surfer only put together a few seconds of decent display.

With his lack of focus, Jay was like a pitcher who just can't find that corner. He was getting up on the board, but his maneuvers weren't crisp, and they didn't link up smoothly. I could see that he was trying to compensate with strength, because the physical dynamics of everything he'd been attempting to do had changed. It was a cascading effect of one mistake immediately compounded by another, over and over. And all of that frustration of not being able to pull off what he knew he was capable of only made him more distracted.

On the long drive home, Jay had to take the full of brunt of my interrogation.

"I gave you a verbal signal," I said. "You should have heard me if your head was clear and there wasn't anything going on. Why didn't it work?"

"Well, I didn't hear you."

"Okay. I gave you visual signals as well. It looked like you were looking at me, but you didn't respond."

"I couldn't see you because the water was glaring."

"All right. What else do you think happened back there?"

"On the second wave, I thought there was somebody paddling right behind me."

"Instead of thinking about where they are, where are *you*?" I asked. "Where did *you* want to be?"

I let him think about it for a minute and then I leveled with him as simply as I could.

You can only compete against yourself.

"You're trying to become the best that you can be," I said. "Every day, every way. You need it to be a mantra. Most people compete against someone else and try to become better than that person, but that's only going to limit you because you'll only be that good. And then what? You'll have to find another to person to compare yourself to.

"It's so much healthier to focus on self-improvement. Have goals, write them down, break them into steps so that you can achieve them, and keep working at that process. What someone else is doing, you cannot influence, you cannot change, you cannot alter. All that data is not useful to you. Do what you can control."

Jay told me he got it.

"Okay, cool," I said. I wanted him to know we were still moving forward, and to keep him excited about it, so I added, "Now we need to work on one maneuver that is distinctively you. One maneuver that you want to be able to do better than anybody in the world. It's going to be something that's attainable for you, that you can manage, that you can set up. So that what other people do is of no importance to you."

It was going to be a lot of training for a kid his age. Aside from the physical work, he'd also have to take an emotional step forward if he was going to progress from being a good surfer to becoming a good surfer who didn't get psyched out at contests. But I knew he had it in him.

We were making some good progress getting Jay's game together as a contest surfer when he told me that he wanted to go slay dragons.

PART VI
SLAYING DRAGONS

PART VI

SLAYING DRAGONS

CHAPTER TWENTY-SEVEN

"I want to learn to surf like you do, Frosty. I want to surf Mavericks."

Jay might as well have said he wanted to put on a blindfold and take dancing lessons on the freeway during rush hour. He was gaining some very decent surfing skillage, but building him up to the caliber of a Mavericks surfer had never even crossed my mind. What did cross my mind was that this fourteen-year-old kid had no idea what he was really asking for.

In those days, Mavs was just beginning to gain legitimacy, and there was only a hardcore underground of people like me who surfed it regularly—and there sure as hell weren't any teenagers in that mix. Now and then we'd get guys from Hawaii and Australia coming to check it out—serious, accomplished surfers who came with a lot of rep—and plenty of them were among the guys I mentioned at the start who would paddle out, have a look, and paddle right back in. Some people couldn't even handle *looking* at Mavericks. They'd wig out and leave. They absolutely wanted nothing to do with it.

Big wave riding itself still wasn't all that popular. Since a lot more people were surfing smaller waves, that's where the surfing industry's attention was, with contest surfing being the main focus. People thought big wave surfing was just too dangerous, and the advertisers and the surf magazines thought there wasn't any money in it. So for anyone who was doing it, it was purely for love. It was a way of life.

At fourteen, who knew if Jay was even ready to *have* a way of life?

Especially one that could get him killed.

I wanted Jay to really understand what the risks were at Mavericks, so I told him about my massive wipeout when I got knocked around by a nineteen-wave set while Steve Ambriel and his Zodiac driver were helplessly watching from seventy-five yards away.

Since even that brutal thrashing hadn't taught me all there was to know about Mavericks, I also told Jay about a day later on when there was a little more westerly pull in the swell and it opened up a really big barrel—and how trying to figure out how to backdoor the barrel and successfully ride it was an endeavor that cost me three boards.

I don't know how many waves I caught before I broke the first one. I had taken off, set everything up, had gotten inside the barrel, and it closed. That's the strangeness of the swell with a little too much west in it; it closes from the front instead of the back, and that tightening mouth of raging water rushes toward you. It's not what you want.

So I got beat. I came off the board, got pulled to the top of the wave and then thrown back down to the bottom. That was most unusual. What normally happens when you wipe out is that your body mass is enough for you to penetrate the wave face, come to the surface as the wave passes the board, and you pull the board back to you by the leash. Then you just climb on, and paddle out of the way before the next wave hits.

When I got tossed down to the bottom of the Mavs wave, though, I didn't penetrate. The water was moving with such force that I got sucked back up the wave and thrown back down again. *That* time I penetrated, and got pushed deep under the pitch-dark water. I was lucky to have had an instant to grab a deep breath before I went under because once I was down there it was physically impossible to swim back up. There was just too much water rushing down on me and I could feel it dragging, spinning, and twisting me in the deep, with no idea what direction I was moving in. Even if I'd been able to swim up, there was no way to tell which way *up* was in the first place.

The forces at play were so massive that the quarter-inch thick leash connecting my ankle to my board got stretched as tight as piano wire. I couldn't pull on it—all I could do was to gently put my fingers to it, waiting to feel it expand so that I'd know that the wave was starting to pass. But suddenly the leash went very slack and I knew something really strange had happened.

When the main energy of the wave had gone by, the board should have floated above me to give me an indication of where up was, but the wave finally passed and the upward pull of the leash was so weak I could barely feel it. Then I got to the surface and found out I didn't have a whole board anymore. The force of the wave had snapped it like a twig.

Being prepared, I had three more in the van. I took off the leash and let the broken board wash in, knowing I could grab it later—hopefully along with the missing half. Swimming in half a mile was enough work without half a board smacking into me. So I grabbed another board from the van, paddled out again, and got thumped again, completely thrashed. Again, I got sucked up the face, pitched over full throttle, sucked under the surface, and broke another board.

After I broke my third board, I thought I should reassess.

"All right, big boy," I said to myself. "This has been a very expensive day. Three boards, $2,400 in just one day. You have one board left, and there are more waves coming later in the week. Figure it out, dipshit: this is not your day. You can't afford to play at this level."

There was nothing more to do but tuck tail, drive into town, and tell Bob I needed some new boards. Fortunately he had some foam in stock because, by then, Clark had started making blanks available year-round.

Really large waves have the potential to change you. And if you surf Mavs on a large day you *do* change—there's just so much energy going on and so much speed and adrenaline that you simply can't go back and surf any other break that same day. It just doesn't work, it feels empty. If you've chosen to surf Mavericks on a particular day, that's where you're surfing. You may as well stay there until you drop.

After I'd busted all those boards, I kept at it at Mavericks until I felt I was supremely efficient at handling the monster waves. When I returned to Mavericks the next season, I had a reputation as an accomplished big wave surfer, and I was very happy with my abilities.

I told Jay that if he wasn't capable of that level of dedication, he'd never surf Mavericks. Then I said, "The first thing is, are you really sure that this is what you want to do? Because the amount of work it will take . . ."

"I want to do this, Frosty."

Most kids—even Jay—don't really know what they're asking when they ask for something like that, what the sacrifices will be. Because there *are* sacrifices.

CHAPTER TWENTY-EIGHT

"To become good enough to surf Mavericks," I told Jay, "you're going to have to bypass a whole lot of what your youth is meant to be. Friendships, girls, parties, chilling, and playing. You're either going to have like-minded friends or you're not going to have friends, because it's not exactly easy to find friends who want to step into the arena of one of the world's largest waves."

"I want to do this, Frosty."

He could be a stubborn little mother, but that's what I liked about him. Like I said, his persistence was phenomenal, and I thought it should be rewarded. Yet at the same time, here's a kid who doesn't have enough life experience to have a clue as to what he is really trying to undertake.

"You're risking your life. You have no idea what you're asking for. As surfers we have a certain exposure to risk, but this is at a whole other level. So I need to know that you're able to hang. That you're not going to panic. That you understand you'll have people tell you that you can't do it, it's impossible, you're too young—whatever it is they're going to say."

Jay just nodded.

"And I have to ask your mom."

That was the tricky part. I always tried to steer clear of Jay's house and his mother because I knew that he wanted me to. He never had to tell me to—that's just something that, if you've been through it, you know it. You know the embarrassment, so there's no need to discuss it.

I'd never had to deal with his mother in order to accomplish what Jay and I were trying to do, but this time I felt there wasn't any choice. I drove out to her place the next day when I knew Jay wouldn't be around.

"Christy," I said, "here's the deal. You know that Jay's becoming a better surfer. You know what my reputation is, you know who I am. And he's now asked me to teach him to surf Mavericks. That's what he wants to focus his training on. I need to ask you if that's okay. I don't know if that's okay. I'm not the parent here, I'm the coach. He's asking for something that is very, very huge. If it's okay with you, then I'll proceed with it. If it's not okay with you, then we're gonna have to figure out a way to dissuade him."

"I thought he was going to be a tennis player," she said, "but he seems to be doing well with surfing, so if that's what he wants to do, sure. Go ahead."

"I have to be very clear here. Bad stuff might happen. Emotionally, I can't be held accountable. I can't have you creating any worse of an issue for me than what I'll already be going through if things go wrong."

We talked it through a little more. At the end of it, she completely understood that there was a lot of risk in what Jay wanted to take on, but that I would give him everything I had to help him become successful, and that I wouldn't take him to Mavericks until I was sure that he was ready.

When I went back to Jay, I laid out the conditions: "I will train you for Mavericks. I will give you everything that I have, but you can't go until I say you're ready. You're asking to become an expert at reading waves. You're asking to become an incredibly good paddler—that's where your success at Mavericks begins: being able to read the waves and catch them. The earlier you can catch them, the better at paddling you are, the more success you're gonna have, because you'll have more control over your situation."

There was one more thing to stress. "You don't have nearly enough data or success in larger surf to be able to make that transition," I told him. "So it's not gonna happen in a few weeks. It's going to be a very, very long transition."

Once again, he simply told me, "I want to do this, Frosty."

*   *   *

Jay became my training partner. It had been easy for me to do what I'd been asked to up to that point, but now I had to really step up my program. Before Jay could even begin the real training, I needed to give him a task that would help him make the transition from kid to adult a lot more quickly than what's normal in our culture.

To undertake the really big challenges, you need to start with a clean slate—what I call "clearing the table." People come with a lot of preconceived notions and misconceptions about success and failure, about how to do things, and about why something can or can't be done. Whether it comes from their parents, the media, their peers, or a thousand other places, so many kids show up with a lot of "I don't measure up" wired into their brains. So you have to cut through that and build from there. You build one block at a time.

For the coach, this means having conversations with the student, listening closely, and picking up what motivates them— what their confidence level is, what their fears are. Then you can begin to figure out how to address that particular person in helping them become successful. You also have to start off with a task where they actually can be successful despite their self-doubt.

Jay came to me with a very clean slate and almost no "I can't." But his fearlessness in the face of Mavericks was a little misinformed. So I needed to clear the table with him by assigning him an "impossible" task that he could succeed at and look back on when things got really hard.

If we'd been on the savannah in Africa, he would have been raised in a tribe, and the tribe's focus would have been how to be successful against a lion. Ever since you'd come into the tribe, you would have been trained in how to deal with a lion. At some point the tribe says, "Hey, now you've got to go out and kill a lion." The unstated message is: "If you get eaten, then we won't have to feed you and you won't be a burden. But if you're successful, as a tribe we'll continue to survive."

The Santa Cruz version that I came up with was to have Jay be successful against Monterey Bay.

"Do you think we could paddle all twenty-eight miles across the Bay?" I asked him.

"I don't know. Can we?"

"People are going to say we can't. They're going to hear that we're planning to paddle across the Bay and they're going to go, 'Oh my God, that's one of those Frosty ideas. You're gonna get lost in the fog, you're gonna be eaten by sharks. You're going to get exhausted and disoriented. You'll paddle out into the ocean never to be seen again.' You know, all the things people can come up with."

Once again: *People are going to tell you something is impossible. They have no idea what's really going on.*

I was working to achieve something that seemed impossible but that we could also break down into parts. People thought it couldn't be done because no one had done it before. It was just all the more reason why I don't want to interact with those kinds of people—and why I've been perceived as being a grumpy old man.

It started off just being Jay and me. We worked through June and July, first paddling a mile and a half from the beach by Jay's street to Capitola wharf and back each workout, then building to four and half, then to nine miles per session. All through the process, Jay was catching a lot of flack from the people that he told about it, but I had a lot of great friends and we ended up with a group of thirteen people when we finally set out to make the trip across the Bay on National Ocean Awareness Day.

*   *   *

One of the people who joined us was our friend Robin Janiszeuf-ski, an ER nurse who lived down the block from Jay. Everyone called her Zeuf. She had had a mastectomy and was looking at the Bay paddle as a way to help bring herself back to who she wanted to be. She entered with some really great safety considerations.

She said, "I think each paddler should have a boat escort and we should each have a whistle and a compass." I was a little taken back because there were thirteen of us and I knew how hard it would be to get that many boats to participate, but the idea for the whistles and compasses was really well thought out, so we made that part of the deal.

Instead of having a boat for every paddler, we ended up with four boats that we loaded up with our gear and enough fluids to stay hydrated for eight hours. We had a compass setting that we were supposed to be following because, even though we were starting out with a high fog, if it became a low fog we would get lost without a compass. Above all, the agreement was that we would be staying together as a group.

We took off from Santa Cruz Harbor. There's a giant marine trench in Monterey Bay that's deeper than the Grand Canyon and runs out for miles. Back in the 1920s, before people knew what deep really meant, fishermen were pulling all sorts of weird species of fish out of the trench that no one had ever seen before. When we came up to the edge of it, we knew we'd made it halfway across so we took our scheduled halfway break. Everyone was supposed to rest up and refuel. This wasn't a race; it was a measured group paddle that we were resolved to do together.

I checked in with Jay, and he was all smiles. We'd made it halfway, he was barely winded, and he was going to accomplish what he'd set out to do.

When the boats started moving again, I yelled out to them because I could tell by my compass that we weren't following the course we had set. Well, I only had a five-dollar compass and the boats had great big fancy ones, and one of the pilots told me, "We're following the setting that's correct."

"Then how come we're so far off?"

"Don't worry about it," the guy said, "we're headed the right way."

What they failed to appreciate is that they were heading the right way for a boat, not for a paddler. They'd chosen to take a course that was closer to shore without taking into account that this had increased our distance, as well as putting us into a headwind. For a boat, what's the difference? You've got an engine and you just use a little more fuel. But for a paddler, it's a pretty damn big difference.

If you're a very strong, highly skilled paddler, you can paddle four or five knots per hour for an extended period of time; we weren't highly skilled or particularly technical, but we were quite capable of covering the twenty-eight miles it takes to do a straight shot across the middle of the Bay. But now we were off course and the boats also ignored the fact that the northwest wind created a current of its own which then dropped down into the trench, hit the wall on the other side, and came back up as yet another current going against us.

We'd already put in four or five hours at this point, and with the currents battling us, Zeuf had reached a point where she was paddling but no longer making any progress. One of the boats stayed close to her to watch how she was doing, and her boyfriend Jackson and I stayed with her as per the agreement.

The rest of the group, though, started moving away. We had been in the water long enough that it had tapped into everybody's fear component. They had become unsure if they could finish, so to make it they were willing to break ranks. Little groups started to paddle off, coming together according to how fast they could paddle, while other groups got left further and further behind.

I was seething. That wasn't the agreement. The agreement was to stick together and finish as a group. I'd given everyone the same training program that Jay and I were following, and if they'd done it they should have had no issues, but even Jay had taken off with the lead group.

So I stayed with Zeuf and Jackson and after a while the guy in the boat said to her, "You haven't progressed in the last fifteen minutes. You need to make forward progress or we'll have to pull you out of the water."

You could see that physically she was tapped. The exhaustion was on her face. Cancer was still impacting her life and her world and she was pissed. But she never broke down, she never quit, and she kept trying to go. With everybody else succumbing to their fears and taking off, here was a woman who had faced fears far, far greater than just paddling across the Bay—and she wasn't giving up.

She was keeping it together and honoring herself. Her body gave out, but her spirit never did.

After another fifteen minutes they said, "Okay, we've got to pull you. You're not making progress. We need you to get in the boat and, Jackson, you need to decide what you're going to do."

To his credit, Jackson said, "I'll get in and be with Zeuf."

Then they looked at me and I said, "I'm going to go catch myself some fucking paddlers."

I started catching up to the different groups and checking in with them. Zeuf's boat went ahead to escort the lead group. By the time we got into Monterey I was with the lead group but I ended making a wrong turn at the last minute and getting out alone at the wrong pier.

When I managed to find everyone, Zeuf and Jackson had already gone. Lake and Roqué were there with Brenda. I took Jay aside because I needed to vent a little.

"What happened back there?" I asked. "You took off on me. That wasn't the agreement. What if I had needed your help? What if you'd needed mine?"

"I'm sorry," he said. "I didn't want to get left behind. I wanted to finish in the lead."

I told him that it hadn't been about that. "If I'm going to make plans that include you, I have to be able to trust you. I need you to be the person I know you can be at all times—someone I can count on. Are we going to have each other's back? If not, I need to know. Because when the shit really comes down, who's going to be there with you? Who really does have your back? This is the stuff that will get you through the really hard times. Are you going to honor yourself and your commitments? It cannot be an unanswered question."

"I will," he told me.

"Good. Now we can get to work."

I left that paddle with such tremendous admiration for Zeuf. I'd seen people who became babbling idiots when they broke down physically. That's not to say that they really were idiots, they just didn't have the discipline and self-control to keep it together. Yet Zeuf had fought cancer, she'd had a breast removed—she'd learned so much more about the challenges that face human beings—and still she had such an indomitable passion for life. I didn't know if she'd been that way all along, or if her own struggles had inspired it, but it was truly inspirational to witness.

CHAPTER TWENTY-NINE

Before Jay attempted Mavericks, I told him, "The only person who can save your whiny little ass is you. You need to understand that, and you need to have a series of plans in place so that as you go deeper and deeper and longer and longer, you never lose sight of what's going on.

"At the beginning you're casual, you just roll on up and get beat. You know that's going to go on, you know you can't swim out of it, and you know that there isn't anything to do but wait while you're getting tossed around. Keep your wits about you. Most wipeouts don't last a really long time ... but then there are the challenging ones. The ones that begin to take you to the limits of how long you can hold your breath. *Your peace comes from knowing you've done all the things that you could have done. That's why you don't shortcut your training.*"

One exercise we did together was to hold our breath while we biked up a 150-yard hill. The rule was, he couldn't cheat and take a breath in the middle, since he wouldn't be able to take a breath in the middle of a wipeout—he had to complete the whole deal.

The reason for it was simple. "If you can take your training to that level," I said, "you're probably going to live. If you cheat, you're probably not going to make it. And it's your choice."

We live in a culture where people don't understand that. Cheating becomes acceptable. I'm a mischievous sort, so I always feel good if I'm shortcutting the system in some way, but there's no shortcut that's acceptable when you're training and your life depends on it.

Jay understood clearly that it was him and him alone. I told him, "I obviously would do anything and everything to come get you, but the reality is that I won't be able to save you. Even though with all my heart and being I would want to, it's not going to happen. If you go down there, the only being that's going to be able to save you *is* you. I know because I've been down there. You need to train yourself to exceed what you think is humanly possible. This is why you train the way you do."

It was one of the issues that I had him write about. He was relatively young, but we needed to approach the subject, because he had to learn not to lose it when the world was coming down around him.

"The first thing you're going to want to do is be afraid and panic. So I have to know what things you're afraid of," I said. "The obvious thing is dying. People are afraid of it. I'm not. Dying is part of living. I was born, I'm going to die, and I have no fear about it. I just don't know when it's coming. All I know is that, when I die, I will not have lived enough."

Jay reflected that he was very unclear about this dying thing and that he had to give it some thought. When he came back to me, he said, "I don't want to die."

"It's not a question of wanting to die. I don't want to, but I'm not afraid."

"Well, I am."

"Then why do you want to surf Mavericks?"

He kept thinking about it as our training progressed. Eventually, he came to understand that it was one thing to have fear, but it was something else to let it immobilize him physically and mentally.

"All of my significant wipeouts have been like getting knocked around by trucks on the freeway," I said. "I was so infinitesimally small. Until you feel that, you don't get it. The ocean is roaring and you're just this molecule in it and nothing you do will change what's going on around you. *You can't deal with the storm when it's at its most tempestuous—you have to wait, and that takes a lot of resolve.*"

A year and a half passed between the time Jay first asked me to train him for Mavs and when I actually let him surf it. I needed his visualization skills to be razor-sharp because of the sheer speed and power involved.

*   *   *

The first time I rode a true Mavericks monster, it was easily a 45-footer. As soon as I got up I noticed there was a warble in the wave that was a little different. I didn't know what that warble meant, but I was there, the opportunity was right, so I took it. I was just getting to my feet when the top of the wave collapsed.

That was the warble.

There was no way out, I was already committed, so whatever was going to happen was going to happen. Fortunately, I'd chosen a good line on takeoff and the wave didn't bounce me. I came out of the whitewater that had crumbled from the upper ten feet of the wave and engulfed me, and I dropped into this completely smooth, contoured wave, setting an edge with the rail of my board. The speed, the acceleration, was absolutely phenomenal. I was practically freefalling—from zero to forty in a second.

With larger waves, everyone has a more compressed stance to be able to stay low to absorb and exert pressure on the rail, and it's also a more aerodynamic position. At zero to forty there's a lot of wind resistance, and if you're slightly off-balance it will blow you right off. It would be like driving down the highway and just stepping out of the vehicle.

So the water was holding the board up, but the board was hurtling downward while I was trying to stand on it as it was dropping away from me. I couldn't believe that somehow I had transitioned out of the whitewater and into this rocking wave that was just *huge*—bigger than anything I'd ever ridden before. Being from the world of large construction, I knew looking down the wave face that it was more than four stories. I dropped so, *so* far. But once I'd done the drop, it wasn't even far enough. It was beyond exhilarating. Every cell in my body was just screaming, *Yeah!*

I'd experimented with several moves at Mavericks, so by the time I'd plunged to the bottom of this monster I knew how to lay out a turn at the speed it was going at. It was crucial for me to do little movements slowly and precisely, because at high speed they have a huge effect. By now there was some bump on the wave as I went back up the face. It got smoother up at the top and I started to ride out its length.

There's a phenomenon that happens for athletes no matter their sport. Visually, they have to process everything that's going on while they're moving at the same time. If you're on a motorcycle and you're accustomed to going thirty miles per hour, and then suddenly you're doing a hundred, can you process it fast enough?

For me, I had to stop processing or get overwhelmed by all the visual data coming in. I had learned long ago that, *You can't process everything, so you need to pick out what you should be focusing on.* So I focused on where I was going. For everything else, I let my body do what it knew it needed to do. My body had had plenty of training in regards to how to turn, where to turn, and when to turn.

When you're dealing with speed, thinking is too slow. So if you've done your visualization work beforehand, you can stop thinking and just let your body respond to all the visual input that is going on.

So I shut it down, finished off the wave, and slid off the board. All I could do after that was float along to let my body decompress and wait for the sensory overload to run its course.

Until I knew that Jay was capable of that level of visualization, there was no way I'd let him take the risk.

In April of 1994, that day had come.

CHAPTER THIRTY

As that second winter of Mavs training was coming to a close, I knew it was Jay's time, but I had to find just the right day. It took until April. The way it turned out, it was going to be the last day of the winter North Pacific large-wave season.

I called Jay up the night before and said, "Okay, it looks like tomorrow's the day."

When I picked him up in the morning, of course the energy and excitement coming off him on the drive up was unbelievable. It was great. It was the culmination of eighteen months of hard labor. I told him again that we weren't going to get right in the water, that we needed to take some time to watch what the ocean was doing.

I'd closely studied the weather system for Mavericks. I had a lot of good data, but I still hadn't seen the water for myself that day. I liked to drive up in daylight and give Mavericks that first hour or hour and a half to let the offshore winds settle down and become more manageable. Then I can see the timing of the sets , how many waves are in a set, what the intensity seems to be, and if it matches my information.

I was explaining all this to Jay as we were driving along the coast about twenty-five miles from Mavericks. Then we came around that curve where you can see the whitewater roaring across the dark surface.

"Well," I said. "Here it is."

It's majestic to be able to see a wave breaking from that far away. Jay kept getting little peeks of it as we got closer, and he got more and more worked up.

I like to park a little bit away from everybody else to have some time to myself before engaging with other people. So we took a little walk on the beach and I gave him our triangulation points. Part of our routine was checking our leashes and making sure there were no little nicks in them before we got in the water, then examining our leash plugs for hidden hairline fractures. As we went through all of our formal procedures, Jay was outwardly calm and collected, but the energy coming from inside of him was palpable. His eyes were wider than ever.

It was going to be a twenty- to twenty-five-foot day. They were already breaking out there. That was small for Mavs, but double anything Jay had ever surfed. And he had earned this—he knew it.

As soon as we got in the water, he left me behind.

I mean, he was *gone*. It was amazing, that enthusiasm of his. While I was still paddling out, he took off on a nice, smallish twenty-foot wave. I watched as he dropped in, and he was completely and totally the kid in the candy store who could eat all the junk he wanted and never get sick. He was just beaming.

He dropped down, made his bottom turn, came on up and got inside, made another turn, and then glided out over the back of the wave. He rode it out all the way and then paddled back into position to catch the next one.

I was beaming myself. It was going to be a good day. There wasn't going to be anything particularly huge, or scary, or unpredictable. The waves were going to hold consistently throughout the day. The tides weren't going to be extreme, the wind wasn't going to pick up. Jay just racked up wave after wave after wave.

Everyone out there that day was like, "Who *is* this kid?" He was just so much fun to have around. He was fifteen. No one could believe it.

He would see people ride and just yell out, "That's a great wave! That's so cool!" He'd get up on a wave and everyone would pick up on his energy. It was a totally great experience for everybody involved. That was Jay's first day. It was the best that it could possibly be.

I knew, "Okay, here's the first step. It's only going to lead to so much more."

* * *

Having hit the water so successfully at Mavericks that first day, it gave Jay enough data to refocus his training. He had all the energy and motivation after that to get ready for the following year. Through the off season, his mind went to work; he had visions. By the time the next season came around he had already progressed significantly from that one day. Then he was off and running.

He had been working with a photographer named Bob Barbour for the last two years and now Bob was very excited about being at Mavericks and finding out that it was legit. There was a world-class, full-on wave in his backyard and he was going to do everything he could to capture it. By working with Bob, Jay was able to look at his body positioning and make adjustments because he could see it in the photos.

It was a favorable season with a good lot of waves coming through, so every time that Jay surfed Mavs that year, he was racking it up. He was recognizing all the little adjustments. We talked about a *lot* of different scenarios. As he began to experience them, he already knew what to expect and how to respond. Then he took his vision to a whole new level. His progress was very quick because we had prepared a very long, diligent path and left nothing unexamined.

He was pumped, primed, and ready.

*   *   *

He was even ready for his first wipeout, which happened pretty early in his second season. It was a mind game. He knew a wipeout was going to happen because, eventually, it happens to everyone.

I watched Jay go up on another twenty-footer, and I watched him go down—hard. I saw the wave pass over him, and Jay's board started to tombstone. It was a 9'8" board and only the first three feet of it came above the surface, oscillating back and forth, rail to rail, because it wanted to come up all the way, but Jay was down below it getting crushed by the wave.

Finally, the board went flat. A few seconds later Jay's head pops up next to it and he's smiling.

He looked at me and, bubbly as ever, said, "That was *okay!*"

"Believe me," I laughed. "They're not all going to be like that."

Jay was going to learn that the hard way—even harder than my way. And, like I said, it almost killed him. But instead, it made him famous.

CHAPTER THIRTY-ONE

Whether you win or lose at whatever you do, you have to take a look and ask yourself, "What value is it, really?" All it should be about is, "Did I achieve the goals that I set out for personal performance?" If you've achieved those goals, regardless of winning or losing, you're progressing. You have to look at it in terms of long-term growth and accomplishment.

If you win even though you know you performed poorly, what have you done? You can be having a tennis match against an opponent who can't make a return. So you can win, but you did not win by performing well. Winning and losing both need to be quantified. *Losing and attaining your goal, that's successful. Winning and not attaining your goal is not successful.*

I bring this up now because Jay had one of the most spectacular failures anyone in the surfing world has ever seen, but he still achieved the most important goal of all.

* * *

From a photographer's perspective, it's a one in ten million shot. The wave itself, the offshore winds, the lighting, the angle the photographer was at in relationship to the board—and sixteen-year-old Jay

Moriarity's arms sticking out with a Christ-like effect as he plunges face-first from the crest of a fifty-foot monster. That's the photo that made the cover of *Surfer* magazine and was in *The New York Times*. It's an incredible statement.

It's also an incredible testament to a monumentally jackass move on Jay's part.

It was late December 1994, and everyone who surfed Mavericks had been studying weather patterns for days. By then, Mavericks was becoming recognized as a legitimate, world-class wave. Some of the Waimea surfers had vouched for it, and they'd started showing up to surf it whenever a great swell was predicted. But it was still largely unknown outside the big wave surfing community.

A notable series of storm systems that produced large waves for an unusually long, consistent period of time seemed to be coming our way. Usually, the significant aspect of a large wave swell is measured in hours, and often it passes in the middle of the night. By the morning you're left with waves that aren't quite big enough to ride. But this one looked like it would come together during the day, and then last for days after that.

I was going to miss out on it because my back injury was acting up again, but Jay could surf Mavericks on his own now, so I knew there was no way he'd skip any part of it.

As surfers, we talked swell all the time. We tried to adjust our days and schedules and commitments to what was coming. We had work commitments, relationship commitments, and all sorts of other things we had to take care of. But what you have to understand is that Mavericks is like a Siren singing from the sea. You're being called. You have to go.

I made sure to give Jay my last-minute advice before the system hit. I spoke with him the night before and the morning of, telling him the same thing both times: Hit the beach early to gather all the information that keeps you from being tempted to go out in conditions that are very difficult to deal with.

I call it the agreement: *Make your agreements before you become emotionally involved, because you don't make good decisions when you're emotionally involved.*

With Mavericks, the agreement means you won't be paddling out when the offshore winds are too strong, delaying your kickoff time in the morning.

I was driving back from work that afternoon when a friend flagged me down on a back road and told me that Jay had nearly been killed at Mavericks. At first, all he said was, "Did you hear about Jay?"

That could've meant anything, but I still caught my breath. Then I said slowly, "No. What *about* Jay?"

"He's okay," my friend said. "But he wiped out at Mavs. It was horrific."

Before my emotions could get the better of me, I focused on listening to the whole story, collecting data, analyzing. Jay had gone down hard and deep, had broken his board in half, but he had survived. In fact, he'd grabbed his backup board, paddled back out, and kept surfing for the rest of the day.

As far as data went, it wasn't much to go on. He'd said the wipeout was "horrific" but I can't stress this enough: *To be successful, you cannot let yourself become tainted by other people's fears.*

Since I knew that Bob Barbour had been at Mavericks shooting for *Surfer*, I drove out to his place and waited for him to develop the pictures so I could see for myself what had happened. As soon as I saw the shots, I knew Jay had ignored my advice. In the sequence of photos, you can see from the way the wave ledged up that the offshore winds had been much too strong to surf in. Jay did everything almost right—except the main thing, which was not to surf until the wind died down.

Jay and I had discussed what he needed to do both that morning and the night before, and he had chosen to ignore all of that. So, sure, I was pissed because he didn't follow the agreement; but I wasn't about to indulge my emotions, because then I would become unthinking, and that wasn't going to help Jay succeed. Even if I did love him like a son, it wasn't my place as a coach to let my feelings affect his training.

He'd be out surfing until late, I knew, so I just waited for him to call me that night and we'd talk through what had happened.

"I had a great day" was the first thing he said. "Did you hear?"

"I heard," I said. "But it wasn't all great. What happened?"

He told me he'd gone out in Bob's boat just before sunrise to save himself the time and energy of paddling out. He had two boards because I'd given him a backup just in case. The fierce offshore winds should have told Jay that it wasn't the right time, but he jumped in the water anyway and joined some guys who were already out.

I had told him what would happen if he went out before those offshores settled down. When the offshore winds are as bad as they were, the wind gets underneath the board and causes a kiting effect, and the stronger that wind is the harder it is to keep the nose down and penetrate through the wave.

But this fifty-footer presented itself and Jay just went for it. He was all full of enthusiasm. "I came here to slay dragons, and here's a dragon, and I'm gonna go."

He said, "Frost, I had to go. It was *there*. I started paddling, felt the wind get under the board and start to kite, but I was already in—there was nothing else I could do. I stood up and right there I knew I was screwed. Then I just dropped and freefell a really long way. I knew what was coming—the rest of the wave was going to follow me down. Frost, *the leash snapped!* I went all the way to the bottom!"

Going all the way to the bottom—the pictures hadn't shown me that.

"I grabbed a good breath," Jay went on, "rolled up in a ball and suddenly I was on the bottom and I was just thinking, 'I don't recall hearing about anyone being on the bottom before. That's new.' I'm doing all the things we had talked about. It was like you said. I just waited. At some point, though, I'd been waiting a really long time."

All he could do was hold his breath and keep waiting, he said. The water was so dark he couldn't see his hand in front of his face. Pinned to the bottom, he at least knew which way up was, but if he tried to swim he would lose even that reference point. While the wave was pushing him down, the current was dragging him along the bottom, and he just kept thinking about how strange it was. At some point, hopefully, there would be the lessening of the downward pressure and he'd get some indication of where up was. Until that happened, he could waste all his energy trying to swim for the surface only to find out he'd been swimming sideways much too late to do anything about it.

There came a moment when he knew he was running out of air and that he still had a lot more work to do. Because of the current, he'd probably already drifted a hundred yards sideways even with the downward pressure. And then there was still the chance that he was caught in a double-wave hold-down: You're at the top of the wave just as it's ready to break and you fall in front of it, so the whole width of the wave needs to pass over you, and then another follows right behind it before you get a chance to surface and catch a breath.

"I had to go up," Jay told me. "But I knew I couldn't force it, so I had to be cool and just tell myself, 'This is it. Whatever happens, happens.' When the wave finally passed, I still had enough air left to swim up to the surface because I hadn't freaked out."

I could hear in his voice that he was proud of himself. His first move had been a poor judgment call, but after that the training kicked in—the biking while holding his breath, the countless essays, the endless evaluations, and, especially, the mental and emotional work. It took a special kind of person to survive that hold-down.

What he ended up with was the most spectacular wipeout of all time, but that was not the most significant part of Jay's accomplishment that day.

Jay was lucky that it turned out to be a one-wave hold-down. He popped up, caught his breath and managed to swim back to the boat.

"I was just like, 'Wow, that was heavy,'" he said. "I swam over to the boat, took off my leash and asked Bob to toss me another board. Bob looked at me like, 'Are you nuts?'"

I know that Bob was still processing the oh-my-God aspect of it at that point. Jay had been under long enough for everyone to get seriously concerned.

"Then Bob just said, 'Yeah, sure,' and passed it over. I took my place in the lineup, and everyone just looked and they were like, 'Dude, wow.' Another wave came and I stroked into it. The wind had died down and it was game on. I was good to go for hours."

"So everything went well?" I asked him.

"I was *on*. Everything was good. Frost, it was wave after wave after wave. I just kept getting to the right place at the right time, being able to set my rail—it was just so cool!"

He was genuinely very, very pleased.

A truly well-known and established big wave surfer had taken a fall in that same set and came up bleeding from a punctured eardrum. That guy was done for the day. And here was Jay having a stellar day after an even uglier crash. He was just putting on a tremendous performance while everyone was asking, "Who *is* this kid?"

This time a lot of people already knew. "That's Jay. He's this kid Frosty's been working with."

I had seen the pictures, and I knew that it would only be a day or so until they got around and people beyond our little surfing community had a look at them. Plus, the weather pattern was holding, so we could expect to have a whole series of days just like this one. Jay's world was about to get much, much bigger, and I wanted to make sure that didn't go to his head.

While I had him on the phone, I asked if there was anything he wanted to say.

"Well, it was there," he said. "And I just—I had to go."

"I know that, but was it the right thing to have done?"

We began to work our way through the process. There are certain waves at Mavericks that cannot be ridden by paddling in— that's all there is to it. I told Jay, "You should have taken more strokes to get down, you should have gotten underneath the lip and you should not have paddled for it until the winds lessened."

You can't look through someone else's eyes, so it was important for Jay and I to touch base because he had to see through his eyes—not mine—why he couldn't have been successful. He needed to do a recap. The most successful athletes don't perceive things as normal athletes. They have a tremendous belief in themselves to pull off the improbable.

From that perspective, Jay having had the confidence to see the wave and assess the situation—knowing the attempt of taking off would be right on the edge of what was possible and then going anyway—it was not a vain leap. It was the result of Jay's training to be capable and successful. No, he didn't make the wave, but he moved forward beyond what anyone had endured for a wipeout at Mavericks, and filled the rest of the day with skillfully ridden waves, making the statement that his work over the last couple of years had been correct and proper.

But it was more risk than a sixteen-year-old should have taken. So we went through his perspective and recreated everything.

"Sometimes you just have to go because it's there, and I understand that," I said. "But you also have to understand the low probability of success—and the risks. If you're willing to live with the consequences of the risk, I have no issue, but you have to really, really understand what those risks are. I want you to have a blast. I want you to surf. Remember your training, how you set yourself up for success, and try to make better assessments."

"I know," he said. Before I could hang up, Jay told me, "Thank you. Without all that you made me do, I never would have made it. Thank you."

I couldn't answer him right away.

CHAPTER THIRTY-TWO

Five days after Jay's wipeout, a world-famous big wave surfer from Hawaii named Mark Foo drowned surfing Mavericks. With Waimea getting more and more crowded and Mavericks finally being considered legit, it had begun to draw a lot of people who wanted to check it out for themselves, especially with a swell coming in that was supposed to last for days.

Mark's death was shocking to the surfing world. He had gone on out on a boat with a group of guys; they saw him wipe out, but they thought he was fine. After that everybody simply lost track of him. The whole atmosphere was very charged up—there was a lot of action, a lot of boats in the water and people shouting. With all of that buzz on the water, nobody was keeping track of each other.

Later in the day things slowed down, and the boats started going back into the harbor. That's when somebody on one of them noticed a broken board. They went on over to pick it up and saw the body. My friend Doc Renneker was onboard. He started working on Foo right away, but it was just too late.

The news traveled incredibly quickly. Nobody knew what to do. The shock was felt not just around town—it was felt around the world. Foo was Hawaiian, from the acknowledged mecca of big wave surfing. He was one of the best in the world, from a place the best in the world went to surf, a local kid who'd done great. It just wasn't plausible. People were in total disbelief that he had gone someplace else and it had taken one of their own.

As is surfing tradition, they honored him by having a paddle-out. The Hawaiians who'd stayed at Half Moon Bay and the Mavericks crew had a ceremony in conjunction with the North Shore crew in Oahu. We all gathered at the base of the cliff at Pillar Point. Doc Renneker gave an incredible speech about the presence of a life force and the glow that a human has. He said that when he first saw Mark's body, that glow was gone.

Then we proceeded for the traditional paddle-out. We paddled into a circle and people were encouraged to speak words of thanks, acknowledgement, remembrance. When that was done there was a pause—a silent prayer—as everyone gathered their thoughts and their energy, and then the noise began. We all shouted out to the sky, hollering and splashing, cupping our hands in the water and throwing it up or smacking the surface, just trying to put out as much sound and emotion as we could. All at once it was a release of pain, an expression of our anger and sadness, and the joy of remembering.

At that moment we were saying, "I am still here and I miss you."

And to the gods we were saying, "Fuck you. You are taking pieces of me but that's all you have. I am here and I count, and you cannot take that from me or those around me. I matter and so do they. My family, my friends—they matter to me. I have left a mark that cannot be taken away. I'm here forever."

Over the next few days it was passed down from the Mavericks crew that they would start keeping track of everyone who took off on a wave from then on. Nobody was going to ride anymore without being accounted for. It changed Mavs from being this real casual place where people were playful to a more serious place that acknowledged the deadly seriousness of the wave.

It was well-intentioned, but I didn't really believe in it because I'd known for years that the forces of nature were insurmountable. Now Jay knew it, too.

"This is why you never shortcut your training," I told him.

CHAPTER THIRTY-THREE

Even before the wipeout, Jay was growing into being a star, and that was very evident to a lot of us. The question was, How big of a star was he going to be?

During that week of surfing, we checked in a lot. He was performing well enough to be noticed by designated world-class people who were saying, "That kid's pretty good. He's pulling off some crazy stuff, and he's very calm."

By having a plan, by having pre-thought situations and knowing what to do, he presented very well. So he was getting recognition from the big wave community. He was putting up enough in the performance venue that, at the end of the day, he was a topic of discussion. And when they interacted with him, they saw he was this unique combination of human elements that made him a really nice guy; they discovered that he wasn't full of himself, and that he was very interested in what other people were doing and feeling.

Outside of that tightly knit group of Mavs surfers, the next people to notice Jay were the surf media. They were hanging around that week, listening to everything and seeing him get accepted into this very elite club. It was a natural fit. He was stepping in with credentials, so it was easier to write about this kid because they'd seen a week's worth of performance. He shined the whole time, laughing and joking as everyone warmed up to him and he warmed up to everyone, forming and cementing friendships.

It was very easy for the media to move forward with him as a darling, because he was. You know, he was *so* young and displaying what maybe only a few others had ever displayed at that age. That confidence and internal comfort—the trained eye picks up all the little subtleties of movement that come from it. Jay had invested all the time and done all that work and that was transmitted through his body, his eyes, and his smile.

Jay was at the heart of a group of quickly rising young Mavericks surfers who were starting to receive a lot of attention that week. Along with Jay there were Peter Mel, Matt Ambrose, and Shawn Rhodes. These were the guys who were going to take Mavericks into the world.

They were the first group of world-class young surfers to give Mavs credibility. Jeff Clark deserves a tremendous amount of credit for surfing it and opening it up to the rest of us, and then there was the very early group that I was a part of, but these kids were becoming the faces of Mavericks. They were starting to do turns in places on the wave that no one had ever considered in big wave riding. They were starting to ride big waves like small waves, with all the subtleties and adjustments. My generation started doing some turns and making some adjustments, but these guys were taking it to a much higher level of performance. And it's gone even beyond that now.

A few weeks after Jay's wipeout, I was suiting up under the nose of the cliff, and when I turned around, there were Jay, Matt, Shawnn and Peter up above me with their boards under their arms, the sun in the blue sky behind them.

I just looked at them and thought: There's the young lions.

They were attractive, people would sponsor them, they were getting a lot of play in the magazines—and Jay was the darling of the darlings because he was the youngest of the young.

Mavericks was fast becoming his playground.

In the months following the wipeout, everything aside from surfing became periphery for Jay. All the media stuff had been a cool experience, but there was no reason to pay much attention to it, because it did nothing for him except open the door to sponsorship—and nobody was stepping up in a significant way. So the attention was nice, but it wasn't yet rewarding in terms of something to be gained financially or athletically.

Jay focused not only on Mavericks, but also on his contest surfing and free surfing, both short board and long board. He wasn't even done with his home-schooling yet, but he was already on his way to becoming a waterman. That was the goal.

When he'd said he wanted to surf Mavericks, that was the beginning of him truly making the statement that he wanted to become a waterman—someone who is capable and confident doing anything in the water. Bob Pearson was helping him by giving him boards at cost and then giving him some clothing and some hats for interviews. He got a sandal sponsor, Flo-Jo's, and he did what most of the guys do when they start off being noticed—got a job at one of the surf shops. Jay went to work at O'Neill's because they would let him take off on notable surf days. As he got more and more recognition, he got more freedom to take off.

Around the time he would have graduated high school, I told him, "To really finalize all that training, you have to go to Hawaii, because they have more competent watermen there than anywhere else. It's a great place to be and you can play all year round. You need to be spending more and more time there, especially during the winter season. You're a top dog here, but Hawaii's still the mecca. When you go there, it's going to take you some time to work your way in, because you won't have the same credibility that you do here at Mavericks."

So I wasn't surprised when Jay, barely eighteen and working part-time, took off for his first trip to this mecca. And I definitely wasn't surprised when I heard how easily and how quickly he managed to work his way in there.

CHAPTER THIRTY-FOUR

The next winter, Jay was back from Hawaii, and we had finished surfing Mavs one Thursday afternoon. As per our normal routine, he went to hang out with the other surfers and the photographers while I went home to my family. At night we would always touch base on the phone and review how the surfing had gone that day. I'd go over the waves that I saw him catch, he'd run ideas by me, and we would go back forth like that, ending the call by talking about what kind of swells might be coming up.

That particular night he said, "Waimea is supposed to break on Saturday. One of the photographers told me there's a system coming."

That was an interesting thing for him to mention, because he hadn't surfed Waimea during his inaugural trip to Hawaii. The last time I'd been to Hawaii was twenty years before, and I hadn't been ready to surf waves that big then. But that had been a long time ago. Before Mavericks.

I'd been working a really intense job and we were just finishing up a very critical stage, so I had some bank. When I got up Friday morning and started to drive to work, I kept thinking about Waimea. Finally, I called in and took off Friday and Monday, then I got Jay on the phone and said, "Would you like to go to Hawaii?"

"Sure! When?"

"Well, I'm going to try to get a flight today and if you want to go, I'll get you a ticket."

When Brenda saw me driving back down the hill in the canyon, she was a little worried because I never came home from work early.

"What's up?" she asked when I came inside. "What's going on?"

I told her what I wanted to do and explained, "This trip is too short notice, and I know the airline's going to gouge me on the price. So what I'll do is take you and the kids another time, but this weekend I want to go for myself."

She said, "You've been buried in work, so go ahead and take a little vacation—go have fun." Brenda was a seriously cool woman.

The airlines at this point would quote you any price they felt like, so I just kept hanging up and calling back until I got a ticket agent who named a price I could live with. It took somewhere between ten and fifteen calls.

I left Brenda the good van and headed out in the truck that I used to make dump runs. When I got to Jay's house he came out with a cool new O'Neill surfboard bag that could carry three boards, plus a giant duffel bag for all the fancy gear they were giving him as his sponsor. We laughed at how different we looked because I had all my stuff packaged in cardboard, bubble wrap, and duct tape that I had picked up at my construction site on the way to Jay's.

We were totally stoked because we'd never made the pilgrimage to Hawaii together. We'd never shared the warm water surfing experience—we'd never even had a surf day together without our wet suits.

Somehow the old truck survived the hour and a half drive to San Francisco, and I dropped Jay at the terminal with our boards while I went to long-term parking and caught the shuttle back. We brought our boards in, but when we went to check in we left them a little bit away from us because we knew they had to go into special baggage.

The woman at the counter asked, "How big are your surfboards?"

Well, we were heading for a swell at Waimea, so some of our boards were huge, but I wasn't going to tell her that and get hit with another heavy charge. So I played dumb, saying, "Oh, they're not very big," and then just started rambling on about Hawaii. There were a lot of people behind us and I was hoping that if I dragged it out long enough she would get frustrated and push us through, which she did.

We gave her our duffle bags and she gave us the tags to put on our boards.

"We'll take them on over to special baggage ourselves," I said. "Just have somebody come out and meet us."

A big Hawaiian guy was there at special baggage. He flashed us a smile as he took the boards and checked the tags, and said, "Have a good time, bra."

On the plane flying over, I told Jay, "You know, it's been almost twenty years since I've been there. In fact, you weren't even born the last time I went. So since you were there last year, you're going to be the driver. Because I'm sure things have changed."

They sure had.

When we landed in Oahu, Jay called his friend Randy Rarick to see if we could spend the night. Randy already had other guests coming, but he said we could crash on the living room floor and that he'd call around for us to see if anyone else could put us up for the rest of the weekend. As we drove out to Sunset Beach, I saw that it was teeming with real estate developments where it had all been pineapple fields and cow pastures the last time I'd gone through. Everywhere I looked, there were surf shops, hotels, and restaurants.

I just kept saying, "Wow, man, none of this even *existed* the last time I was here!"

And Jay just kept laughing and driving the car.

As soon as we got to Randy's house, we could hear the waves. Randy and his wife came out and Jay made the introductions. They were so excited to see him.

Randy asked, "How early in the morning do you want to wake up?"

I was like, "Randy, I don't even know if we're going to be able to sleep."

"Well, when you guys called I thought I'd do a little checking, and everyone is kind of split about whether the swell is going to be big enough for Waimea. From the sound that I can hear, it's not a Waimea swell yet. More could come, but it's not big enough yet."

"Hey, it wasn't forecast until tomorrow and surfing Sunset is a treat anyway, so we win no matter what."

All through the rest of the night as we lay on the floor trying to sleep, we could hear the intensity of the waves building up out there. Just after dawn, Randy walked us down to Sunset through a little path that the locals used. The surf was alive with large, beautiful waves. Jay and I could hardly get over how great it was. It was gorgeous and warm and we were walking around in shorts and flip-flops. It wasn't like home at all as we watched these amazing waves just roll in one after another.

Randy said, "Well, it's not really a Waimea swell, but there's some size here. It'll be good."

We just hung out watching the waves for a few more minutes—then a set came in.

When Randy saw it, he said, "Boys, this may be your set. That set broke at Waimea. That one was it. So we might as well go over there and see what's up."

"Sure," Jay said, "we're game."

We jumped in Randy's car and drove on over. There was a crew gathering at Waimea when we got there and, since Randy knew everybody, he started introducing us. Some of them had heard of Jay and started giving him kudos and telling him they were excited that he had come over. Meanwhile, we were looking at surfing what, by Waimea standards, was a medium-sized swell. It was on, it was happening.

After about fifteen minutes, a double-set came in.

"It looks like you guys got lucky," Randy said. "This should carry through until the afternoon, and then it's probably going to back off a little bit."

We went back to Randy's house to grab our boards and while Jay was inside meeting more people, I walked back over to Sunset to watch the waves. A crew was getting together there, too, and I even ran into some surfers I knew from way back. While a few of us were reminiscing and talking story, I was seeing more and more sets. I was started to get the jones then—I wanted to get in the water.

When Randy and Jay came back, Randy introduced us to a guy named George Downing, the master forecaster.

"The real sets start at 10:05," he told us. "This'll last longer than people think but I'm not sure if it's going to go into tomorrow."

It was about 7:30, so I looked at Jay and said it was time for us to get going.

We unpacked our boards and loaded them in the rental car. When we got over to Waimea again, we realized we didn't have any wax.

"This'll work out fine," I said. "There's a couple of guys in the water. I'll watch them and see if they know what they're doing while you go get the wax. By the time you come back, I'll have figured out what we should be doing off of these guys."

A couple of sets came through while Jay was gone, one of significance, and I could tell that the surfers I was watching knew the setup. When Jay got back, we waxed up in the grass, walked down to the sand where the channel was, and a lifeguard on the beach started heading our way.

"Let me talk to him," I said. "He's going to be worried about who we are and whether we can we handle ourselves, because he's the one who'll have to rescue us if we don't. It's a bummer for him to have to get in the water."

Jay is all slicked out in his O'Neill gear, while I'm wearing the neon I'm-a-Dad baggies that my kids bought for me. We weren't tan because of the wet suits we usually wore, so everything but our faces and hands were milky white—plus I was wearing booties because I'm not used to surfing without them. I could certainly understand why that lifeguard wanted to check us out.

"Hey guys," he said when he got over to us. "How are we doing?"

"We're doing well. I bet we're quite a sight to you."

"Well, actually, you are."

"I used to a be lifeguard," I assured him. "So I appreciate your concern."

He nodded, not particularly convinced. "Where are you from?

"We're from Northern California."

"Okay, do you surf large waves?"

"Yeah, we've surfed a few. We've got a clue as to what's going on."

"Have you been to the islands before?"

"We both have," I said, "but it's been a little while for me."

Eyeing my booties, then my baggies, then finally my face, the lifeguard asked, "So where in California do you surf?"

"Mostly around Santa Cruz."

"Santa Cruz?" He paused a moment. "Do you guys happen to surf that big place near Half Moon Bay?"

"You mean Mavericks?"

"Yeah!"

"We do."

"Then have a great time," he said. "If it stays good, I'll come out and join you when I have a break."

Having satisfied the lifeguard, we dropped into the channel and paddled out to where the two guys had been joined by a third. In Hawaii, the locals usually wait until later in the morning for the trade winds to pick up and improve conditions. It was too early for that, so most of the locals weren't out yet, which was great for us because I knew it was rare to have a chance to surf Waimea without a crowd jockeying for every wave.

I was trying to set up my triangulation when Jay just suddenly spins and goes. A few minutes later, I was still figuring out my plan and saying good morning to the other three surfers when he came paddling back out with that big old grin on his face, saying, "This is so cool!"

Another wave came and Jay took right off again as I continued to get a lay of the land and a feel for how the water moved. When he came back out the second time, the game was on.

When I started taking waves, Jay and I were out of sync, him paddling back while I was riding them in. The waves were consistent enough that we could keep catching them one after another, but we couldn't sync up. We were just giving each other a smile and a nod as we passed each other by. Finally, there was a break in the set and we ended up back outside together, reviewing our waves.

"I went for a little barrel and got thumped," I said, "but I made a few. How cool is it to be able to open your eyes and see the turbulence of the water? At one point I saw it coming and it was like, 'The wave's passing you! You need to come on up before the next wave comes and grab a breath of air, dipshit!'"

We started laughing and Jay said, "Yeah, I got that barrel on the inside, too! It sets up sweet."

"Yeah, you get in there and you do a big cutback and kind of draw it out," I said. "But as soon as the barrel sets up that opening, you have to do a little back-off to be able to get out the end before you hit the shore pound on the inside and get *totally* thumped."

We surfed for probably another three hours before it started to get more crowded and we weren't catching any waves.

"Let's take a break," I said, "grab a bite to eat, give someone else a shot at these waves and we'll come back later. This will be a great time while we're chilling and relaxing to go check out some other breaks, so let's get some food to go."

We grabbed some food at the local market, stashed our boards at Randy's, then went to check out Pipeline, which many claim is the most perfect wave anywhere in the world if conditions are right. Waves never get as big as they do at Pipeline. The waves were triple overhead and perfect.

Pipeline is a left barrel, and the whole idea is to be able to disappear from view, finish the wave, pop back into view, and kick out. But it can be so hard to catch the drop-in. Sometimes the guys were freefalling on their drop-ins and reconnecting with the wave at the bottom, but they'd be wiggling because now they'd gotten off balance, and they would eat it with the lip of the wave slamming them in the back. On the other hand, some of the guys would squeak enough of a bottom turn in to be able to pull into the barrel, and when they did, it was just spectacular.

After maybe forty five minutes, I turned to Jay and said, "This is not working for me. In my head, I'm surfing every one of these waves with these guys. I'm expending as much energy sitting here watching as what I'd be doing in the water. I'm going to go buy Brenda and the kids some gifts. I'll come back and pick you up in an hour or so."

Jay just laughed and said, "Yeah, okay, old man."

So I drove into town, bought a really nice dress for Brenda, picked up a tie-dye T-shirt for Lake because he was into those, and got a "Hawaii" T-shirt for Roqué.

When I picked up Jay he said the swell seemed to be changing.

"Okay, well let's go back to Waimea and see what's happening," I said.

There must have been 150 guys out in the water by the time we got back. It was way more packed than it was reasonable for it to be. As usual, there was the pit crew—the guys who were totally dialed-in and catching all the bombs—and there were at least thirty of them. This was the mecca, so everybody from everywhere was out there scrambling for waves.

"Maybe we should go on back to Sunset and check that out," I suggested.

Jay, he was like the Cheshire Cat, his grin was so big. He knew he was sitting on top of the world. He was like, "Frost, man, I'm in Hawaii and I'm surfing in large swell—it doesn't *get* any better."

Well, we got to Sunset and it was putting on a quite a show, so we grabbed our boards at Randy's and headed back to the beach. As we were walking to the channel, I knew there was something that I needed to remember about surfing Sunset. It was kind of a weird break with a lot of oddities to it, but it had been such a long time.

"I know there's something about paddling out," I told Jay, "but there's *really* something about coming in and I don't remember what it is. Well, I'll figure it out."

When we got into the water, I said, "I know where I want to go surf. There's the inside bowl, and then there's a break, and then there's another bowl. I have a particular liking for this other bowl that picks up water, because the water moves just like it does back home. So that's where you can find me."

Of course, Jay took off. He was a much better paddler than me, having surfed Sunset last year, and he had a wave of his own that he liked. So he was happy.

Meanwhile, I was curious because I had been riding a tri-fin, but I also had a single-fin that I'd gotten made special by Glen at Rainbow Fins that I wanted to test out. At Mavericks, the waves are often not consistent enough to be able to repeat a wave to the extent that you can find out how a board will react to it again and again. With the waves always changing, it was difficult to make any comparison. Bob Pearson and I had been testing board designs at Mavs for years, but, because of how much the Mavericks waves differed from swell to swell, we were always left with the big question: *Is it me, or is it the board?*

So I was pretty confident in this tri-fin because I'd been riding it for a while, but I also had this single fin I wanted to take out because both the tri-fin and single-fin boards were designed to be identical. I was really curious as to how the single-fin was going to feel in a wave like Sunset that is so perfect time and time again.

I paddled out past Jay and I saw he was already in a little pack at one of the outer reefs. He was getting into a conversation with Ken Bradshaw, a champion big wave surfer who was about my age—a lot of the guys Jay's age had posters on their bedroom walls with Ken surfing a sixty-footer. So I figured that was going to get interesting.

Once I started to catch waves, it was perfect. I was on an experimental, test-fighter board that I was somewhat familiar with; the waves were awesome, and the trades weren't too strong. You can get kiting under your board in Hawaii, but, because things are a little different there, the wind is usually only blowing hard enough to make the wave that much cleaner and better.

Ken definitely considered this to be his territory. I saw him checking me out, but I was on, I was doing well, I wasn't embarrassing anybody, so I figured it was totally cool. And it was. We had a great session. We surfed until almost dark. Then I took my last wave.

I lay down on my board in the whitewater to head on in and, once again, I'm going, "I know there's something I'm supposed to remember. I know there's something I'm supposed to remember! What's the deal about coming in at Sunset?! Oh, I remember! I'm not supposed to be going this way—there's a reef here!"

Next thing I knew it was, crunch, crunch—*rip!* And then it was too late. The reef tore the fin right out of the bottom of my board. It was a fine time to remember.

There was no way to find the fin—I wasn't even going to try. There was no sense in worrying about it. That board was done for the trip.

Jay was sitting on the beach laughing his ass off when I came out.

He said, "Dude, I thought you surfed here before!"

"Yeah, yeah, I did, man. Don't grind it in."

No matter what was happening, Jay would laugh. He was the perfect surf partner. Obviously, he was not like me.

PART VII

LIVE LIKE JAY

CHAPTER THIRTY-FIVE

I had gone surfing early on a Sunday morning in April. It rocked, it was totally cool. There were great waves, the sun was out, and I came home completely pumped. The kids were out front playing, and I asked if they'd had breakfast because Brenda liked to sleep in on the weekends. When I got into the house, I saw that Brenda was already up, so we started talking while I got myself something to eat. Brenda was telling me about something she wanted to do that afternoon when her speech began to slur. I turned and looked at her. Her face looked fine. Then she spoke a little more and I watched as one side of her face suddenly slumped.

I'd seen the same thing happen to my father.

"You're having a stroke," I said. "We need to go to the hospital. How do you feel?"

Brenda thought I was crazy. "I feel fine," she said. "I'm not having a stroke. Everything's fine. I just went to the doctor two weeks ago and I couldn't be better."

"Okay," I said, "but you're having a stroke. Let's get you to the hospital and get you checked out." I called out to the kids and told them to get in the van.

Brenda, being Brenda, insisted, "This really isn't necessary."

"I know what I'm looking at. We have a couple of doorways to go through so be careful and let me know if you need a hand. Once we get outside, I want you to put your arm around my shoulders and I'll hold onto you. If we get to the van and nothing more happens, great, but I want to get you to the hospital—now."

As we walked across our yard with her arm around me, I could feel her body start to give out. I asked Lake to open the passenger door for me, and I got Brenda turned around. She still had enough control to sit down, so I strapped her in.

Starting up the van, I thought of calling 911, but I knew I could get us to the hospital faster. In a situation like that I knew it was crucial to get care as quickly as possible, and I also wanted her to get real care, so I headed for Dominican where Lake and Roqué had been born and Brenda and I knew a lot of people.

I told Lake I'd be driving right up to the front doors. "What I need you to do is not to listen to anybody, just do what I tell you to do. I will walk in and grab a wheelchair and call out, 'My wife is having a stroke.' That will prompt people to move. I need you to open up the passenger door because I'm going to be moving pretty quickly, and close it after I get your mother into the chair. Then you and your sister follow me inside and find a place to sit down. I will be back with you as soon as I give them information I need to give them."

Medical personnel showed up as I was getting Brenda into the wheelchair. Once they'd gotten her inside, I told them everything that had happened.

"She was speaking clearly, then she started to slur her words," I said. "I looked at her face and it was normal, and then it just started to slump. That's all the information I have."

They started going through the procedure of treating a stroke victim, so I said, "I've got two kids over in the waiting room. It's time for me to go to them if you have everything, if not—"

"No, go deal with them," a nurse told me. "We've got enough information for now."

I told the kids that their mom was having a stroke and that I knew exactly what was going on because my father had had one. They didn't have to worry, I said, because we had responded so fast, and that even if she had to be in the hospital for a while she would be okay.

"I have to talk to the doctors some more, but do you have any questions?"

They were in shock. They had no idea what any of it meant. With Lake being eight and Roqué only five, there was nothing they could do but worry, so I called up my buddy Everett to come and get them. "I will stay with Mom until later in the evening and then I'll pick you guys up so that you can get ready for school tomorrow."

Everett and I were still working for the same company at the time. When he came and got Lake and Roqué, he told me, "Take care of Brenda. You don't have to come back to work until you're ready."

Monday was not a good day. The doctor said that rather than having a stroke, Brenda had had an aneurism. A blood vessel had burst in her brain and her brain had hemorrhaged, so they'd had to cut a hole in her skull to relieve the pressure. I knew the surgeon who had done it and I knew how awesome he was. The nurses that I knew assured me that he was as good as I had heard, as good as you could get.

But Brenda was still unconscious after surgery.

I went back to the house, got the kids up and off to school, went back to the hospital, and hung out all day.

On Tuesday Brenda could respond to my voice. When I would speak to her and hold her hand, she was able to squeeze it. The doctors and nurses were all very reassuring that Brenda's condition was getting better. So I thought, This is going to be totally cool. We're going to be fine.

Toward the end of the day, a minister came into the room. She was a wonderful woman in her mid-forties who was quick to let me know that she was just checking in. "I'm not here for anything," she said.

Since things were looking up, I went home and talked to the kids about what we were going to do that summer. Brenda was going to be recovering and going through therapy, and what we were going to do was be part of her therapy team. We would rub her arms and legs and take her for walks. At some point, she would be able to go for bike rides, and these were all things we could do with her to help with her recovery.

People recovered from strokes, I told them. Sometimes it took a few weeks, sometimes it took many months, but we had a plan. And even though we were already a very close family, with their mom in a time of need, I said, it would bring us even closer together.

"This will work out just fine," I told them. "Our deck is an awesome place to hang out in the summertime. We can do more barbeques. And, Roqué, you're starting to swim, we can take Mom to the beach and you guys can get in the water with her. This will be totally awesome."

On Wednesday, things did not look good. That was a big hit. But as far as I was concerned it was only a stage, just another part of the healing process. Brenda had made real progress the day before, and sometimes the body just didn't come around the way you wanted it to. At worst, I thought Brenda's recovery might take a little longer than I'd hoped for. No one was giving me any dire reports.

Later that evening the minister came back. She wanted me to tell her about Brenda.

"I'm very proud of Brenda," I said. I told her we had been married nearly nineteen years. I told her about how we went to dinner every Friday night, how she had gone to Goddard because she didn't like the pressure of taking tests, so she found a college where there were only term papers and no exams, and how cool it was that she'd gotten around the system—just a lot of little stories about who we were as a couple and as parents.

When I left that night I still hadn't been given any dire predictions.

On Thursday morning the surgeon said, "We need to talk."

It's never good when someone says that. All I could answer was, "Okay, sure."

Then he told me. "Brenda is dead. We've got her on life support, but there's nothing more we can do."

It was unfathomable. I can't express the power of that statement and how it just wiped everything blank. There was no way to process it. It was no place where I was. I'm an incredibly positive person. I will find the positive in every situation, and I believe in the power of that. But I couldn't even think. I had no reaction. If breath and pulse hadn't been automatic, I would have died there and then because there was nothing—there was no process going on inside me.

After a while, I just said, "I don't understand. I know what you said, but I don't have any ability to—how did this happen?"

"With some people, this is what happens. This one just worked out that way."

If I didn't know how skilled he was, I would have called his abilities into question, but I knew going in that he was capable and competent and that he would have done everything humanly possible. Those are pretty stellar endorsements to default to when the world falls apart.

He asked if I wanted to keep Brenda on life support. We had already talked about that for both of us and that was not how either of us ever wanted to live.

The surgeon told me, "The only reason that she has any functioning organs right now is because we have machines that are making that happen. If you've already given thought to this, have you given thought to what to do with her organs?"

"Yes, we have. If there's anything that can be given to anybody, please do that."

The donation people had a representative there with lots of paperwork to sign. She said I could deal with it later, but I just wanted to get it over with.

"I don't want to have to come back here," I said. "I have two kids at home that I'm going to have to explain this to, and I have absolutely no idea how I'm going to do it. So let's just get this taken care of now."

She told me that because they had kept Brenda functioning, all of her organs were still in good condition. They had a thirty-five-year-old mechanic in Denver. They were going to send a team to remove Brenda's heart by that afternoon and have it implanted in the man by that night. If it took, Brenda's heart would be in a man who had a wife and two children.

I said that that would be a tremendous honor, to be able to be that helpful.

As I was walking out of the hospital, Bob Pearson was there. He said, "I heard." He asked what he or anyone could do to help.

"There's nothing right now," I said. "I just want to be left alone. I don't want anybody to show up, I don't want anybody to do anything. When I'm ready, I will come out. I just want to be alone with the kids."

"Okay, I hear you."

"And please have people understand, I'm not ready to deal with them. If anybody comes by, I'll take the kids and we'll be gone. I don't want to do that. I would prefer that we have time to figure out our lives. I know everybody wishes the best, but right now I have to be with the kids."

So I left and got them. We went and sat on the couch and just cried. Gut-wrenching, I know that term. My gut tightened up and I couldn't breathe. I was crying and gasping for air. And I was cold.

For Lake and Roqué, I have no idea what their comprehension was. I explained it, but there's explaining and then there's comprehending. I don't think that they could understand.

My process was just to cry and cry and cry. We cried for days.

When I could think again, my first reaction was, "I have two precious kids who don't have anybody but me. I cannot expose them to the loss of another parent. So, I can't go to work, I can't leave their side, I need to keep them here with me, and we'll just stay in this house."

I remembered that when Roqué had been three, she somehow cut her finger and started to bleed. You and I understand that that's no big deal, but Roqué didn't. Here was this stuff coming out of her skin that she didn't understand. She was leaking. She just looked at Brenda and me and said, "Am I gonna die?"

"No, Precious," we told her. "You're going to be fine."

Now she was five and I was trying to explain to her about her mother dying and no longer being there, not because she wanted to die, not because she didn't want to be there—because she certainly did—but that it could happen, that your body was only good for so long and then eventually we all passed. It was all age appropriate, what I was trying to explain, and I knew that, as Roqué grew older and understood more, she would ask more questions. It would take a long time to evolve through that.

We didn't have a funeral, we had a wake. That was something that Brenda had talked about. She wanted her passing dealt with as a celebration. We did the best we could. There was a restaurant that Brenda and I went to as our end of the week tradition, so I asked if we could celebrate her passing there. They very generously said yes. We shut the place down. People from work, friends, and all the people that would and could showed up and we celebrated her life.

Jay was invaluable in all of that, because I was there, but I was not. I was so out of it that I recall very little of what happened. I do remember seeing Jay when I arrived, and then at some point he pulled me away and said, "It's time for you to go."

It wasn't a place for me to be drinking. I appreciated the participation of so many wonderful people, but I couldn't even begin to remember what happened other than that Jay was there. He had called beforehand and asked if I wanted him to bring me. I had told him that I was okay.

He took care of me as best he could. When it was time for me to go, he made sure I was able to drive and took me outside to collect myself.

Over the next few weeks, I really thought I was going to lose Lake. He was nine years old and he and Brenda had been so close. When he was younger, I had carved a tiki from a redwood tree that was on the property and put it at the bottom of our driveway. It had the big scary tiki face on top and a heart at the bottom of it. When Lake asked what it was, I had told him it was there to ward off evil spirits and keep us safe.

We were picking up our mail at the top of the drive a couple of weeks after Brenda passed. Lake looked at the tiki, he looked at me, and he said, "Well that didn't work, did it?" Then he turned away and walked up the drive.

CHAPTER THIRTY-SIX

We had to begin to put our lives back together. With the kids there were just lots and lots of conversations about living and dying and relating. We started slowly moving forward.

They had to go back to school, and I couldn't stand being home without other things to occupy my mind. At home, all I wanted to do was to dwell on Brenda's passing, and I could only do that so much. I returned to work after two and a half weeks and told the guys on the construction site, "I'm here. And I'm here because I have to have something to distract me from where my mind wants to go. I have to have the discipline to be on a job site and be safe, but keep an eye on me because I'll flash into a whole other space. I need you guys to take care of me instead of me taking care of you right now."

Though I'd been hoping that the distraction of work and the ability to return to focus and stay focused would help me get through my process, Brenda's passing was just too awful a blow.

There was a surf contest that I traditionally entered that was coming up. I thought going to the beach was probably going to be a good thing for me to do, but I needed to stay away from people. A friend had brought Lake and Roqué down to the event, and I told them I'd be near the rocks over by the cliff and that they could come hang out with me, but I wasn't focused enough to watch them. Mentally, I still wasn't there.

My body runs hot so I usually wear a much lighter, thinner wet suit than most people. When I got in the water, though, I had never been so cold in my entire life. It was sunny and everyone was walking around in their shorts and I got out and bundled up in a towel on top of the suit, but I was still freezing cold. I tried to get focused enough to take part in the event, but all I can remember is how cold I was, my teeth chattering and my body shaking there on the rocks. It was a long time before I was functioning and able to surf freely.

After being at work a few weeks, I was beginning to be able to focus for most of the day. After a month, I could do it for the whole day. Brenda was in my thoughts all of the time, so it was a real challenge. But I was eventually able to focus, because focusing is a habit.

When the summer came, I sent the kids to the east coast to be with their grandparents and the rest of their family. Before they left, I started to change the house. I put in all new furniture and I asked Lake and Roqué what they wanted, because I couldn't live there anymore without making very significant alterations.

Once the kids were gone, I dropped half the house—just cut it away with a chainsaw—and added an extension to give the place a whole new look.

Still, I couldn't get back to myself.

Two years before Brenda passed, I had been in a car accident where the woman driving the other vehicle had died. At the hospital, one of the responding officers had told me that the police saw no responsibility on my part.

"I just killed a lady," I said. "There's not really a whole lot you're going to be able to tell me that's going to make me feel any better."

"It's going to be hard," the officer said. "But you'll come through this. There wasn't anything you could have done."

About a year and a half after the accident, Brenda came to me and said, "When am I going to get my man back?"

I had put enough pieces together by then to realize that I held all the answers. In going through it all, I went to a priest who I found completely inadequate, then to a minister, who was almost as inadequate, and then to a rabbi. None of them were capable of giving me anything to get me through.

They just kept telling me, "This is God's way. It will pass." Well that was just absolutely not nearly enough for me. It gave me no solace, no peace in my heart.

I thought, "I'm a caring, responsible human being and everything I believe in has just been turned upside down. And you give me powder puff answers? How could you even begin to believe that that would get a thinking human being through a situation like this? You have no touch with any sort of reality. I don't know what you do, but this is serious shit. You didn't even bring a knife to a gunfight—you gave me a paper airplane."

That's when I looked inside long enough and figured out that the only person who could help me was me. I already knew that, but my belief had been shaken because I thought that I had been living a correct and proper life, and so things were supposed to go my way. Things were supposed to be getting easier, not harder. Here I was trying to live a peaceful, respectful life, and I'd killed someone.

I had to reexamine every aspect of my life, of who and what I was and how I lived, and get rid of the parts that were questionable. I had to be real clear with myself about staying true to who I was.

I told myself: *Either you are who you live to be, or you are not.*

Six months later, Brenda was dead.

The kids would be home at the end of the summer and I had to be there for them—all of me.

I began to accept that life was going to be whatever it was going to be. I couldn't do anything about my fate. All I could do was live my life and be true to who I was. I had always maintained that I believed in myself and in my capabilities and that, somehow, some way, I would always come through.

Something was telling me, "Now you're being called. Either you're going to be who you said you are, or you're going to have to fold and your life has been false—it's meant nothing."

And because I do believe in me, I answered, "Okay, you're calling me out and I'm calling you back. I am who I am, and I will live to be who I have always said I am. Because my life has not been a lie. I don't know how, but I will figure out how to be me, to honor what I've always represented and come out the other side. Because I am that strong."

I became very aware that I was a person with a mind, and what you learn in athletics is that the mind is very easily manipulated. You can convince yourself that a lot of things you're doing are right and correct. But you're supposed to use your intellect to be sure that you are true to who you want to be. The way you measure that is with your heart. And so, if something feels good in your head, that doesn't necessarily mean that it's good. But if something feels good in your heart, that's the true test. If your heart is unsettled, if your heart is disturbed, if your heart isn't feeling right—your heart doesn't lie.

When the kids got back from their grandparents, I told them, "As you go through life you need to listen to your heart. Develop your minds, but it's your heart that will guide you. Use that as your compass so you keep going in the direction you should be going."

Even so, it took years for us to truly begin to heal.

CHAPTER THIRTY-SEVEN

While the kids and I started putting our lives back together, Jay had started to put back together the relationship with his father, Doug.

We were in my van catching up and he told me, "My mom said my dad is coming to visit."

For the Army to let him go on leave was a big deal, and Jay had a lot of excitement and angst about meeting up with him again for the first time in so many years.

"I'm really nervous," he said. "This is really strange. I haven't seen him and there was a long time where I didn't know anything; I didn't know what was going on. Now he wants to come and visit. I want to see him, I want to know my dad, but I don't know what's going to happen."

"Well," I said, "that's honest. That's probably a good thing. We're not gonna make a judgment because we don't know everything that went on. But here's an opportunity for you to have a relationship with your father. And if you can grow it, that will be awesome. But like any relationship, it will have its awkward moments. So just give it your best. Go in without having premade any judgments or decisions, because everything you've heard has been filtered through your mom, and I will tell you that I don't really have much good to say about my ex. I try to be fair and honest about her, but my heart was broken, and when someone breaks your heart you end up with a huge blind spot where they used to be. It's only now that I have enough life experience behind me to say that we were both very, very young.

"So that's coming from me. Your mom and dad went through something similar. There's a lot of bitterness that comes out of that. But this is your father, and your father is entitled to have a shot. Give him a shot. It would suck to look in the mirror and say, 'I didn't even give him a chance.' That's a pretty hard thing to live with for the rest of your life. So give him a chance. Then you will be a person of honor. Because if you don't, if you walk in already having made up your mind, that's not fair."

"I hear you," he said, "but I just don't know how it's going to go."

"You're not supposed to know. This is a big step. He's got to face a whole lot of things to come back and see you after all this time. You're going to face a lot of things, too. What are the two of you going to do?"

"I really don't know, Frost."

"Let me give you a suggestion, okay?"

"Definitely," Jay said.

"It's going to be uncomfortable and awkward, so you should find a place where you'll both be comfortable so that there's nothing making the situation more difficult. Trust me that your dad's going to flip if you do it at your mom's house."

"Yeah, I can totally see that."

"Go down to the beach. That's where you're the most comfortable, that's your element, and your dad's a ranger so he's good with the outdoors. It's neutral ground not associated with Christy. He'll appreciate it."

Jay perked right up when he heard the idea. "Yeah," he said, smiling. "This is going to work. This'll be good."

"And keep in mind, if it turns out to be hard to relate to him at first, cut him a little slack. Everybody deserves that. Understanding that is part of being a man. You're not always sweetness and light yourself. Sometimes you can be really obstinate and hardheaded."

The grin shined on. "*Me?*"

A couple of days after Doug's first visit, Jay came back to me totally stoked and said, "My dad's so cool, Frost!"

"He should be. He's done a lot of cool stuff in his life."

"He wants to come visit again soon. I'm really looking forward to it. He even used to surf."

Jay was beaming. I told him, "That's awesome, Jaybird."

"Do you know he's got kids? I mean, I've got these half-brothers. They've seen me in the magazines and they want to learn how to surf. My dad's going to bring them down to the beach and I'm going to teach them!"

Once Jay found out that he and his dad were going be cool, it was game on. They were off and running. It turned out that the Army had transferred Doug from Panama to central California, so it was much easier for him to start building a relationship with Jay. Suddenly having this whole new family was so exciting for Jay, so when Doug came back with his wife and kids, they were welcomed into the neighborhood.

It was a surf day, which meant that there were crowds of people everywhere. I sort of hung back while Jay was introducing Doug to all his friends, starting with Zeuf and Boots McGhee. Doug in turn was making the introductions for his wife and kids. He was a very gracious guy—he liked to shake hands.

Jay was giving his new brothers a surfing lesson later that day when Boots introduced Doug and I on 36th Avenue overlooking the ocean, where Jay lived, saying, "This is Frosty, Jay's coach. He taught Jay how to surf."

We just shook hands and Doug said, "Thank you so much for working with Jay."

I told him, "You're more than welcome. He's a great kid. And he's on his way to becoming an incredible human being."

It became very apparent that it was difficult for Doug to meet me, and somewhat strange for me as well. But I would never be Jay's father. I am who I am and I was comfortable with that.

When Jay got back, he was telling his brothers how well they'd done and also giving them pointers on how they could improve. I couldn't have been happier for him, or prouder. And of course he couldn't wipe the smile off his face. He shared my philosophy that you always want to let somebody end an interaction on a positive note.

When he said, "You guys did really good out there," I picked up on the followup.

"Did you have a good time?" I asked.

"It was awesome," one of the kids said.

Jay grinned. "They were totally cool."

One of the things that Doug did, being in the Army, was parachuting. So Doug asked Jay if he would be interested in skydiving.

Jay was just all over it. For him it was, "This is on—let's do this."

After they did it a couple of times, Jay said to me, "This is totally cool, totally awesome. What do you think?" I agreed, it did sound totally cool and awesome, but when he said, "Well, let's go together," I knew I had to back off.

I had to tell him, "No, Jay, that's not for me."

"But, Frost, man, you'd really like it. It's such a rush. It's just like surfing Mavs. You jump out of the plane, and you've got to reach the point where you've jumped enough that they let you open your own shoot, and then you land, hustle up, and you go do it again."

It would definitely have fit within my lifelong process of addressing my fear of heights and thrill-seeking, but it was the one thing that Jay got to do with his dad. I really felt it was important for me to let them have something that was special and unique between them.

You know, I'm sure for Doug it was not nearly enough, but it was something he alone got to do with his son. I knew that it meant a great deal to him, so I wouldn't involve myself.

At first, Doug was footing the bill for the skydiving excursions across the bay but, Jay being Jay, he wanted to become exceptional at it, which meant he needed to do it more often than his dad could. So it was hysterical watching Jay trying to talk his surf buddies into going with him.

A lot of them, even the Mavs surfers, just told him, "Jaybird, why would I want to jump out of a perfectly good airplane?"

"Dude," Jay would say, "that's the whole point!"

Some of the gang did end up becoming skydiving enthusiasts because of Jay. Part of that was because no one in the crew wanted to be outdone. More than anything, it was that Jay's enthusiasm was so contagious—infectious.

Still, I never did get in on the parachuting. It would have been gluttonous if I had. There were so many other arenas where I got to hang with Jay.

CHAPTER THIRTY-EIGHT

About a year and a half after Brenda passed away, I was at Pleasure Point getting ready to go surfing when Zeuf walked by. I took a look at her, and I was just like, "Oh, wow, she's pretty cool."

I'd never forgotten how much passion and honor she'd shown during the paddle across Monterey Bay. She'd been friends with Brenda and me, and with Jay and my kids, for several years, but that's all there had been to it.

When we had all started seeing a lot of each other, Brenda had once asked me if there was anything she needed to be concerned about. Now, I'm naïve on a lot of levels, so I asked her, "What do you mean, should you be concerned?"

"Is there something going on between you and Zeuf?"

"Good lord, *no!*" I said. "Do you know how hardheaded that woman is? She won't change her mind on anything. She's worse than me!"

Brenda knew when I took that tone and started talking about "hardheaded" that it was all okay. For me at the time, to even think there would be something between Zeuf and me was just unfathomable. She did not shy away from any argument, and when she thought she was right she'd put up her case. When that happened, you'd better have your ducks in a row or she'd blow them out of the water.

The first time I met her she'd been out surfing with a girlfriend at Pleasure Point. They were laughing and having a really good time, and not everyone figures out that surfing's supposed to be fun. So I paddled by and said, "You know ladies, it's great to see you having such a good time—good job."

A few days later I was checking out the surf before paddling out and this very attractive woman walked up and said, "I want to thank you for your comment the other day."

Well, I make a lot of comments to a lot of people, and they're not always all that wonderful. I asked her, "What comment was that?"

"You acknowledged that my girlfriend and I were having a good time and that was nice of you, because it's obvious that you're a very good surfer and we're not, so it was nice of you to be that encouraging."

I told her, "Oh, you know, no big deal. Like I said, it's great to see people having a good time. Not everyone knows how to."

It turned out she'd recently moved to Santa Cruz, so she ended up at a party that Brenda and I were at. When I introduced her to Brenda, I wasn't sure of her name at first because it's kind of confusing. It's spelled Zeuf, pronounced "Zoof," and my hearing sucks, so I thought she was saying Zeus as in the Greek god.

But we kept ending up at the same parties and running into each other at the beach. A friendship started coming together. She was incredibly intelligent, and our exchanges became a little more interesting every time we had a conversation.

When Roqué turned three, Brenda and I said, "It's your party. You get to invite whoever you want." Well, shocking to us, she had this whole list of adults along with kids that she wanted to have there, and Zeuf was right on her list.

When people started showing up at the house on the big day, Roqué got very serious about the introductions. I remember her saying, "Zeuf, this is my friend Tia Di. Tia Di, this is my friend Zeuf."

I mean, it was so formal, and everyone was watching Roqué go through this scenario that she had envisioned in her head. It was hilarious. Then she looked at her wrist as if she was wearing a watch and announced, "It's now time to do the piñata."

When I looked over at Brenda and Zeuf, they were in hysterics at being puppets in Roqué's little playhouse.

Now, a few years after Brenda's death, I was a bit shocked to realize that I wanted to ask Zeuf out. But when I'd see her at the beach and she'd ask how me and the kids were doing, I couldn't help noticing her tall, athletic physique, her lightly bronzed skin, and her surf- and sun-streaked blonde hair. Or how she came alive and her eyes lit up when she laughed.

After our first dinner date, I went to pay the bill because the way I was raised, that's what a guy's supposed to do. But she looked at me, and said, "That's quite all right. I'll pay my share."

I started laughing and I was like, "I don't think so!"

"Nope."

She was just so independent. I think I managed to prevail on that one, though, and buy her dinner. That's how the relationship started.

She was fascinating. We never took the same course to get to whatever decisions we'd make, but so frequently we'd get the same result. It would always crack us up—we didn't understand each other's reasoning, but we ended up trusting that we'd usually end up at the same place.

It took a bit of time, but she was someone that I'd already known and who I had great respect for. I had dated a couple of women, but dating was totally weird. Brenda and I were almost at our nineteenth anniversary when she passed. We'd been married a long time. So when I started to date, I figured, "I know that I'm a handful, not easy to deal with, so there's no sense in pussyfooting around. I'm just going to be me. I'll give you a full dose of who and what I am; if it won't work, let's get it out of the way quickly."

I didn't think I had much of a chance of being in another relationship because I'd already been in a successful one and I had very high expectations. Plus, I already knew how disastrous a bad relationship could be.

Yet it moved along really well because Zeuf and I already had this great friendship. I already knew her integrity. Before long, the only question remaining between us was that of lifestyle compatibility. Zeuf's job was intense. She was a critical care nurse who had worked in the hospital in Oakland where gang shooting victims were regularly taken. Now she was working the night shift so she could surf during the day and have a life. She had this nice little arrangement all set up, and then I came along with the kids.

Since they already knew her, when I told them I was dating Zeuf, they said it was cool. Then we started hanging out together as a family. It seemed to work fairly well. Zeuf was taking Lake and Roqué to the beach and teaching Roqué how to swim. So we decided to move in together.

I had the house in the canyon, Zeuf had a house at the beach, and I was not too thrilled at the prospect of ever living at the beach because there's way too many people dropping by. It's like living in a fishbowl. I'm very protective of my privacy and my alone time. I love spending time with friends and telling stories, but to have random people dropping by just because they happened to be surfing in your neighborhood was not something I was into.

Then I got to see a whole other aspect of Zeuf because we were hanging out so much. There were not a lot of women surfers at the time, so Zeuf was a touchstone for all the female surfers over by

Pleasure Point. These girls would come on over to have conversations with her. She was ten or fifteen years older than they were, and she would give them advice about how to surf, how to dress, how to deal with boys, school, parents—just backing them up and supporting them.

Of course, I was very psyched about how Zeuf was working with and encouraging the up-and-coming young female surfers. So it would be contrary to my nature and background and what I believe in to say, "Let's pull you away from the access that people have to you now and put you up in the canyon where people cannot get to you."

The logical place for Zeuf was Pleasure Point. And, suddenly, it was the logical place for me. That created a new dilemma for me, because it meant I was going to be in town and around a lot of people when I might need space just to spread my arms and breathe.

My solution was to tell Zeuf, "Okay, here's one of the deals. If I grab the kids, leave you a note, and say I need a break, it will have nothing to do with you. It will just mean I'm too fenced in with too many people around me, and I need some space to breathe. If I ever have an issue with you, I'll let you know. But I don't know how living in town around all these people is going to affect me."

Our street ran right to the cliff at Pleasure Point, and there were literally hundreds of people walking up and down it on a daily basis. That was going to be a big, big adjustment for me. What I didn't know was that the vast majority of those people would leave after six, and then it was just our little neighborhood. And we had an incredible neighborhood. There were so many awesome people and we'd get together at the spur of the moment. We'd just be walking down the street, and see two or three other couples and say, "Hey, let's have 'cue. Whose house are we going to have it at?"

Then it was like, "I've got some steak" and "I've got some ribs," and "I'll bring some fish." And we would just put together an impromptu meal. Sometimes, I'd say, "I'm fixing some Irish coffee," and then I'd brew up a batch based on a recipe that it took me a year and a half to steal from this place in Delaware. But you need to gauge how much you can have, so I serve quarter-sies, half-sies, and the full deal, because they'll kick you.

It's a rocking neighborhood. People drop fish off when they have excess from their catch and then we'll distribute it. Our friends have fresh vegetables from their gardens that we spread around and most of the other people do the same with whatever they have. It's great. I'm thrilled they let me in.

Jay had been stoked when Zeuf and I started dating because he'd known her since she moved into Santa Cruz and she was one of his favorite people. Once we were married, it was even better because we were just a few houses down from his place and he was in our lives every day. So he had plenty of friends around to help him celebrate the day he set a surf record that stands to this day.

CHAPTER THIRTY-NINE

Surf-O-Rama was a Pleasure Point contest that drew surfers from as far away as Hawaii and Japan. The conditions on the day of the 1999 event were fantastic—glassy, with head-high frost and solid-medium glide. And Jay knew he was right at the top of his game. Just watching him paddle out and get into the lineup on his first heat, I could see he had no issues. He was calm, he was enjoying himself, and his focus was razor-sharp.

Everything went his way. Waves just seemed to come to him. Jay did everything he could possibly do with style, power, and grace. From arching to making his bottom-turns and cover-ups, then waking and making it through. He stepped it up and started going into nose work, hanging five, hanging ten, doing complete roundhouse cutbacks, rebounding off the whitewater, and coming back around and getting through more sections, with a prominent display of body language and trim. He demonstrated a complete mastery of the board and the surf.

Throughout the day, he won every heat. Not only did he win them, he crushed the competition, scoring three perfect tens. The contest was a solid representation of the talent that was around, so to dominate the whole thing was quite a statement. There'd been a number of very notable players at Surf-O-Rama through the years—Bob Pearson, Wingnut Weaver—who had done particularly well, but they'd never dominated a contest the way Jay did with his three perfect tens in the final. It had never been done before, and it hasn't been done since.

It was such a pleasure watching Jay surf.

After he scored that final ten, he was ecstatic, as he should have been.

When he came out the water, I told him, "You did a great job, Jay. I want you to think about it and we'll talk in a few days."

When we spoke again, I asked him, "How cool was that? You've been judged as having been perfect for three different waves. You surfed them all a little bit differently. All of your interpretations must have been perfect because you got all tens. How does that feel? What do you think?"

Where I was going with it was, "Was that the best you could surf?"

In posing that question to him, it was so he could recognize that, no, it was not perfect. On each of those waves there were areas where he could improve, and significantly improve. We don't surf for other people, we surf for ourselves. When you do something, you want to do it the best that you can do it. Regardless of what the perception of perfect is, you know there is room for improvement. When you're good, you're striving to find all those little nuances where improvements are possible. The more you learn, the deeper the layering goes.

That's what a coach has to illustrate—that there's mental work that needs to go into a deeper understanding of what the athlete should be seeing. The coach needs to be bringing the athlete along intellectually so that their progress on that level accompanies their physical evolution. There's never an end.

After Surf-O-Rama, Jay became even more passionate. It was a motivator for him. He got very excited and refocused and reenergized. He wasn't lacking anything before that, but now he was like, "I can see what you mean. As good as it was, I can see the fault in it."

The better you become at something, if you're observant, you can see how many more things you could have done to make your performance even better.

That became a real motivator in his life. When he was surfing, he surfed long and hard; when there was no surf or he needed a break, he worked out in different ways. He got the deal. The better conditioned he was, the more he could remove the questions as he found himself in sketchy situations; the more prepared he was, the more he could count on his conditioning to pull him through.

For all his skillage and conditioning, though, it still wasn't providing him with an income that he could count on. As Jay got older, this became more and more of an issue.

CHAPTER FORTY

It was June and Jay came by the house because he was getting ready to take off on his summer work deal. O'Neill had him running a surf camp in Europe where people would sign up for lessons and go spend a few days surfing in Norway, Scotland, France, Portugal, and wherever. He had been doing that for a couple of years, so he came by because we'd been talking a lot about his future lately. He was very curious about finding out what he was worth financially to the surf industry, because he was using surfing for his livelihood. He was starting to have real adult concerns because he was almost 23, he had just married his girlfriend Kim, and he was thinking about how he was going to live his life, how he could afford to do the things he wanted to do. He didn't want to have to live hand to mouth.

So he said, "Can we talk?"

"Well, of course we can talk."

He was like my son and had become an older brother to Lake and Roqué. We sat down in the combination kitchen-living room, discussing what he was going to do over the summer, and talked about getting together in the early fall to work out and start prepping for Mavs.

"Frost, man," he said. "I'm not making a go of it. I get next to nothing for this surf camp thing. It's fun to do and they pick up all my travel, but, for me to be able to train and have the freedom to go surf big waves when they happen and spend the season at Mavs, there's no money. Nobody's come forth with anything other than product, and product doesn't do me any good unless I go sell it. Isn't there a better way?"

Jay was on the Greg Noll surf team by then. Greg is the grandfather of all this, the premiere big wave rider, acknowledged for having ridden the largest waves until the modern era. Jay had met him on our trip to Hawaii, and Greg's prowess at Waimea was the stuff of legend. He was in a whole different realm, yet even he couldn't figure out how to get significant sponsorship for his team. The industry was still transitioning from small contest sponsorship to noticing that the media was starting to do a lot more big wave coverage. The sponsors didn't know yet if there was any money in it. Despite the media, they couldn't figure out how to capitalize on the attention.

I had many, many other things to do, and working on the sponsorship angle wasn't going to be one of them unless Jay found himself completely stymied. He had other friends who were more connected with that part of the surfing world and they should have been able to set him up if anything was even available. In terms of professional sports as a paying gig, surfing was so far down the list it was pathetic. So, even though Jay was still a darling, he was struggling.

I didn't know any sources to tap into for sponsorship. I had told Jay early on, "I don't know the people to be able to put it together for you."

You have to remember how single-minded Jay could be. While it was frustrating for me not to have an answer for him, it was much more frustrating for Jay.

"That's not what I want to hear, Frost. I have to get this worked out. I just want to be sponsored. It should be so easy. I need a vehicle to go to Mavs that isn't duct-taped and wired together. Kim's folks have a cabin and I don't know if my truck can even get there. I can't even buy gas for the boat to go water skiing. Forget about taking Kim out for dinner. Everyone is doing all these things that I can't do."

"I'll try to talk to some people before you get back," I told him. "We need to establish what your value is. Or you can align yourself in the surf industry and try to become a product rep, but there are demands on that. If you're a rep, no one's going to be thrilled if you take off and go surfing and you don't fulfill your commitments to sell product, supply product, and babysit all the areas where it falls apart. Some people make a lot of money doing that, but they don't get a lot of time off."

Jay shook his head. "Then that wouldn't really work out for me. It's just been bugging me and I can't let go of it. I mean, am I being ripped off? Am I being fairly compensated?"

He had been looking at others and hearing rumors of what they were being paid.

"That's why we need to talk to some people who could tell you the honest truth," I said. "Why listen to rumors—to some dipshit who doesn't know what they're talking about?"

"I don't want to worry about this anymore," Jay said. "I don't want this eating at me the whole time I'm gone. It sucks."

"So let's talk alternatives so you won't keep having these sleepless nights. I got into construction because, if you watch your money, you can work seven months and you might be able to do part-time for the other five. You can make enough that you get to do what your passion is. But there's no extra money. Look," I said, "I hear your concern and it sucks, but now that you're making mature decisions and considering a future—that's the big deal. How long are you gonna grovel with no one giving you any money?"

Again it went back to, "I just want to be sponsored."

At that point, Lake and Roqué came in from playing and Roqué hopped right up on Jay's lap. Nothing changes the feel of a room like kid-energy, especially for Jay. He started telling them about his big summer trip, and that he would be stopping in the Maldives.

"That's a kind of island that's called an atoll," he explained.

"What's an atoll?" Roqué asked.

"It's a ring of land with water in the middle and the ocean surrounding it. The water in the middle is called a lagoon. The water's warm, the air's warm. It's almost at sea level so, when the storms come in, everything gets wet. I'm going to go diving and look at all the different fish."

He knew that would grab them because they'd gone snorkling in Hawaii and had returned armed with all sorts of fun fish facts and anecdotes.

Then the kids started filling Jay in about their adventures swimming out to the kelp beds with Zeuf and how their surfing was going. Roqué was already a little style master without even knowing it, while Lake was more of a stand up and charge-through kind of guy.

"How was it at the kelp beds?" he asked Roqué.

"There was lots of stinky kelp."

"That figures."

"And I saw some otters."

"Awesome! So what are you working on with your surfing?"

"Doing trim," she said.

With that, Jay lifted her off his lap and stood her in front of him, saying, "Oh yeah? How's your footwork? Show me your crouch."

Roqué went into her stance.

"That looks good," Jay said. Then he reached out and adjusted her arm. "But try it like this."

When it was time for the kids to go do their homework, Jay slumped in his chair again.

"I'm stressing," he said. "I come back with next to no money. There's just nothing there. I come back with nothing to get me through the winter."

"You made an obligation, so you can't back out—you need to keep your word. If you made it through last winter you'll make it through the next one. It's not going to be comfortable, it won't be easy, but now you know about looking into the future and making plans. I'm guessing that you're not going to be doing this next year. You've got new considerations, and you want more in your life than just the struggle of trying to find two nickels to rub together."

"I know, that's why I'm stressing."

"It's my job to point out the choices you have," I told him. "But the decision has to be yours, because you have to live that life—not me. I made my own choices. I saw that some wouldn't give me any of what I wanted, while others would give me some of what I wanted. I don't think anybody ever gets to choose an option that gives them everything."

"Yeah," he said, "it's cool."

I got up and said, "Listen, Jaybird. Just go have a great time and we'll deal with the rest of it when you get back. Everything is in motion for you."

Finally, Jay smiled. He had heard enough to know that there was a process happening. He gave Zeuf and me a hug and we walked him to the door. As he was going out, he said, "Okay, I hear you. When I come back, we can work on coming to some kind of a decision."

He waved and smiled again.

"This will go away," I told him. "We'll find a solution."

"I'll see you guys when I get back," he said. "You have a good time."

I never saw him again.

CHAPTER FORTY-ONE

One of my fondest memories dates back to the first summer after we'd moved in with Zeuf. There was a swell coming and the kids said they wanted to go surfing. I told them, "Okay, if it's small enough when I come home from work, we'll go surfing."

Of course when the time came, I took a look at the beach and the surf was roaring. So I said, "Hey you guys, it's way too big for me to take you out and to feel comfortable about the two of you being in the water. I'm going to go surfing and we'll do something when I get back."

"No," Roqué insisted. "You said you were gonna take us surfing."

"It's not safe and I'm not going to take you out."

They were bummed, and still were when I got back.

I never talked to little kids like they were little kids, especially not my own little kids. "Guys," I explained, "I want you to have a safe experience. You're precious to me. I don't want to do something that's going to jeopardize your enjoyment and stop you from having a good time."

"But you said!"

"But I have to back down from what I said if it's not safe. The swell's bigger than I had anticipated and—"

"But you *said!*"

Well, it was hard to pierce the logic of their argument, so I took a look at the models, which said the swell was going to drop for the following day. I knew it was still going to be larger than what I felt comfortable with for the kids, but I said, "All right, you guys are such smartasses, you want to go ahead and go in? Tomorrow when I show up from work, we'll go surfing. Be ready, because we're doing it."

They told me, "*We'll* be ready!"

Next day, I drove home, listened to the buoys, and it was definitely going to be larger than I was comfortable with. Zeuf had been working with them on their swimming and they could both easily go half a mile in the ocean. They knew what to do in case they got into trouble—how to be cool and think their way through the process of getting back to the beach without panicking. But the thought that they might be needing that training didn't make me happy.

So here come the three of us with our boogie boards, all wetsuited up and our fins hanging, and there's Jay and a couple of his buddies sitting on the bench at the end of the street on top of the cliff.

Jay came over and said, "Frost, it's pretty big."

"The kids said they want to go and they made a big deal about it. They said they wanted to go regardless."

"Do you need a hand getting them out?"

"I think we're going to be okay getting out, but keep an eye on us if you would."

Before we got in the water, I talked to Lake and Roqué about how we were going to approach swimming out and how we were going to use the channel and time the sets. We waited as we got our fins on and timed a set until it was finished, then we jumped in the water and all three of us kicked on out with no problem. I remember little Roqué kicking like crazy up this five-foot face and over the top.

We caught some waves, but I could see that there was a real look of concern on each of their faces. Their eyes were really large and darting around, paying super close attention. This was not a casual go-out for them. They knew they were definitely pushing their limits.

Jay could have gone surfing, but instead he was hanging out keeping an eye on the kids. When we started coming in it was difficult because we couldn't see what was coming up behind us. We were trying to stay together and catch the same wave to get to the beach at the same time but that didn't work because, as soon as we caught one that would take us in, Roqué got bounced out.

Since Lake was older and more experienced, the only choice I had was to flip out of the wave and go back for Roqué, hoping that Lake could make it all the way in on his own.

It would have been a truly frightening decision to make, except that I knew Jay was up on the bench, watching over his little brother while I went back for Roqué.

The two of us caught the next wave and, as we started riding it in, I could see Jay directing Lake to where he needed to land to be able to take off his flippers and get up the rocks. Roqué and I came in just behind him and the three of us maneuvered through the rocks and got to the stairs—the socks Lake wore because his fins were too big were slogging off his feet, and all three of us were panting, covered in sand and foam.

Jay was at the top of the stairs, doubled over with laughter.

"You guys are a fine picture," he said, mussing Roqué's salty hair.

Then we all started laughing and went back to the house for dinner.

CHAPTER FORTY-TWO

A couple of weeks after Jay took off for Europe, I went mountain biking with a pal of his named Mikey G. Aside from being a Mavs surfer, Mikey was a serious mountain biker, and I had progressed enough to ride with his crew, so I was in really good shape. I rode from my side of town to Mikey's place, which was a seven-mile warmup. I was used to that and still completely stoked to set off on our ride, but we were only half an hour into it when I suddenly lost all of my energy.

For a moment, I was completely unable to function.

I didn't know what to do. We were heading up a particularly steep pitch that I always looked forward to because it was challenging. We weren't even a quarter of the way up when I called to Mikey G. and said, "I'm done."

He stopped and came back and asked, "What's up, Frost?"

"Mikey," I said, "I don't understand it. I'm completely drained. I'm done. I've got nothing left in the tank."

Usually, we went from two and a half to four hours, depending on how much time we had, and we weren't even an hour in. I hadn't been pushing it or anything. I was flabbergasted, just didn't know what to make of it.

"I've got to ride home," I told him. "I must be getting sick. I'm really sorry, I apologize."

"You want me to ride with you?"

"I should be okay."

Mikey told me, "I'll ride with you."

I couldn't believe how exhausted I was. It took a real effort to get home. I didn't comprehend it at all.

The next day I felt much better. It was a Saturday and I'd promised the kids I would take them camping, so off we went. It was just the three of us because Zeuf had to work.

We stopped at the market in Carmel to pick up the last of our groceries and ice, and then drove the hour and a half south to Big Sur. When we got out of cell phone range, I turned the thing off. It was me and my kids hanging out where a 3,500-foot mountain range looks straight down at the sea, and I wasn't a big cell phone person anyway.

That night we built a fire and made s'mores, camping at a site right on the edge of the mountains overlooking the ocean. We were having a great time, laughing and joking around and being together. On Sunday morning we drove down the mountain to a gorgeous little bay called Sand Dollar Beach. It curves gently into the base of the mountain, and the slope isolates it from the rest of the shoreline on either side. The water is always brutally cold, with rocky gray and green islands sticking out of the bright blue surf. It's a place that Brenda and I had really enjoyed going to.

We stayed there for a couple of hours, then we drove home.

As we were approaching the end of our street on the cliff, I could see this mass of flowers. It was wider than the two-lane street, and the flowers were stacked up from four to six feet high.

There's thousands upon thousands of flowers and I'm going, "Wow! Somebody decided to sell flowers at the beach. What a great idea!" And I'm just beaming, telling Lake and Roqué, "That is so cool! I hope they make a lot of money because what a nice display. I know they can't sell this many in one weekend, but how gorgeous."

I saw a bunch people milling around and I thought whoever was selling those flowers must be doing great business.

I had parked the van and started to unload it while the kids were putting away their stuff when I saw two friends of mine coming over, Mike Curtis and Don Curry.

I was in such a great mood. I called out, "Hey, guys! How you doing?"

I'm waving, I've got a smile—someone's selling flowers at the end of my street and life is wonderful.

Mike looked at me and said, "You don't know, do you?"

"Know what? The kids and I have been camping. We were grooving and having such a great time I decided not to even turn the cell phone on."

Mike said, "You don't have a clue."

"Mike, what are you talking about?"

"Frosty, Jay's gone."

I just looked at him. I said, "Mike, what do you mean?"

He said, "Jay drowned."

I said, "That's not possible." Then I began to cry.

"It's real," Mike told me. "It's true."

Mike and Don gave me a hug, then we sat down and we cried together. Lake and Roqué came over and I had to tell them. We all cried. I was back behind the van and I just walked into the house with my kids.

In the doorway, I turned around and told Mike and Don, "I hurt." Then I closed the door and stayed in the house.

I couldn't deal with anything more that day. It took me until Monday to go to the end of the street to take a look at what was there, to read the messages that people had left, to see the display of love, respect, and caring that so many people had for Jay.

It was nearly a week before I could get all the information.

As Jay had told me, he had gotten the opportunity to go to the Maldives in the Indian Ocean for a week or two to surf some very special breaks. He was hanging out at a surf camp on an atoll and had decided to go free diving.

To this day, the details are very sketchy about exactly what happened. At some point, the other surfers just noticed that he wasn't around anymore. They said, "Oh, he's probably diving. He's working on conditioning. We'll check on him later."

They found his body at night.

What had happened on that bike ride, according to all accounts, was that my body had broken at the same time Jay was underwater, blacking out. For me, I can only imagine that he was calling out in some way to tap into my energy.

When Jay passed it hit my heart hard. And I was tired of getting hit. I'd been hit too hard, too often, and I lost passion for just about everything. I especially lost my passion for surfing Mavs. It brought back too many memories, too much of where I lived and where I had hoped to be and what I had wanted to do. Without being able to see Jay there, it just wasn't the same. It felt empty.

I felt robbed. I felt cheated. Jay and I were supposed to have a relationship that lasted a lifetime—we could have had thirty or forty years to know each other. I can't express what a shock it was to have that ripped away.

My parents were one thing; you expect your parents to go before you do. It's not out of order. When Brenda passed, it was completely unanticipated and devastating. For her parents to have one of their children die before they had, it was inconceivable. My relationship with Jay was so close that that's the only thing I can equate it to. It was out of order, unnatural, and unfair.

That is not just from my perspective, but from a greater one because of the impact he was having on the world. He had grown into being an ambassador for the surfing lifestyle. There were only a few people who had made that transition. Greg Noll was one, as was Rell Sun, and Jay, with his smile, his graciousness, and his presence, was going to be another.

When he worked with people, they just felt better. People who had only met him briefly took an immediate interest in him and what he was doing. He was able to get past people's prejudices and disarm them. He was granted this special spot because he had such a big heart. He could have altered so many people's lives. So many people I talk to now say, "He did it for me. He got me interested in surfing—and so much more."

When Jay was gone, I had to find my center, my balance, my peace all over again. I didn't talk about it for a long time because I was trying to find myself. I was trying to find how this utterly horrible event fit into the order of life.

* * *

On the day of the paddle-out, I still didn't know exactly what had happened to Jay and I was still in shock. The impact that Jay's death had on our community was unbelievable—not only in Santa Cruz, but up and down the coast. I remember going over to what had been Kim and Jay's apartment. Kim, Jeff Clark, Bob Pearson, and I started the walk from there, leading literally hundreds of people down to 36th Avenue where Jay had grown up.

The road was packed with people that had to separate to allow us to walk down the stairs to the beach. That whole side of town had shut down. I was a wreck, tears flowing down my cheeks, and every face in the crowd was streaked the same way. They were so respectful, opening up to let us through, throwing flowers, and trying to let Kim know they all wanted to support her.

When we got into the water, we were joined by hundreds more people. There may have been over a thousand people. They had paddled their boards into a formation of concentric circles in the bay. Zeuf was one of the paddlers on the sixty-foot outrigger canoe that brought Jay's ashes to the center of the circles, Dave Dyk was the steersman, and Boots carried the urn.

Boots passed the ashes over to Kim, who was sitting on Jay's favorite Maverick's board. Kim took the urn and slid down into the water. Then she swam under to release the ashes back to the ocean.

I know that people said their goodbyes, their words of grief and celebration, that we threw water to the sky and cried out in love and pain, but I could not believe it was happening.

Kim put Jay's ashes in the water. That's most of what I remember.

Then there was another ceremony at Mavericks after that. The Mavs crew paddled and formed its own single circle. It was an overcast, miserable day, although the water was glassy. Everybody held hands and said their goodbyes. People were apologizing for being jerks. They acknowledged that Jay was such a special person, someone they wanted to emulate. They promised to step into living new and better lives.

I couldn't speak because there was too much to say. Once I got started, where would I stop?

When the last goodbye had been spoken, Kim looked around the circle and said to everybody, "Take a look at the formation of our circle." Everybody was still holding their position because the circle represents a wholeness, a continuum.

Everybody had been so wrapped up in their own emotions, so absorbed in trying to find some purpose for being and honoring Jay's passing that no one had noticed how the circle had morphed.

We all looked around stunned, saying, "My God. How? How did that happen?"

It wasn't contrived. It wasn't intentional.

The circle had morphed into a heart.

* * *

It wasn't until some more of the hazy details of Jay's accident started coming through, and people were trying to piece together what had happened, that I began to emerge from the ice-cold fog I felt I was moving through. I'd gotten worn down, tired of getting hit by life, and I needed to recharge the batteries and take a break. It was a pause, a deep breath, and a reevaluation.

When Jay had gone missing, it had been inconceivable that anything had happened to him because, by that time, he was perceived as somebody who was completely invincible. The feats he performed—other people didn't even try them because it was such hard work.

The more I thought about it, I realized it was not that important to me to know precisely how Jay had died, because I knew so intimately—and was so very proud of—how he had lived.

I know that I've pushed it too far many, many times and I have been very, very fortunate. When people make the choices they make in living their lives, death is one of the consequences, whether you want to acknowledge it or not. But just because you *can* die doesn't mean you should stop doing what you do. It's part of the reason some of us do what we do. It's exciting to live a little bit more on the edge.

Yet, I don't think that was a motivating factor in anything Jay did. He wanted to do something that people had not done before, and he was very excited at being able to be beyond competent at what he was trying to do. It was the work itself that drove him.

Whether Jay went too deep or too far, he wasn't doing it to show off—no one even *saw* him dive. And he didn't do it for thrills. Jay did things simply to become better doing them, all the time. Being beyond competent, that *was* the thrill.

That's why I'm so adamant about the fact that, in our culture, we don't recognize the value of giving young people a notable, definitive event to make the transition from being a kid to being an adult. We don't have to send a kid out to slay a lion, or even to paddle across Monterey Bay, but people truly need some type of event to be able to help them get through the sleepless nights—to have something to look back on and say, "You know what? *I* did that."

We need to give young people the opportunity to do things that are larger than what they can envision.

In life you have a choice: Either you're going to continue on, or you're going to stop right there—your growth is going to stop; your exposure to things is going to stop. Your passion, your joy, your progression are all going to stop. Because life continues whether you're taking part in it or not.

Somebody asks me, "Hey Frosty, how you doing?" and I tell them, "I'm smiling." I know how sucky it can really be and what a great life I get to live, what great family, friends, and experiences I've had. It rocks. Does that mean it's been easy? Not at all.

I've managed to give some people enough background to help them meet all kinds of challenges. It's about the most gratifying thing in the world to be the person in someone's corner saying, "Yeah it sucks, it really does, but you can get through this."

It's a choice. If you want to go ahead and quit, you can call it off, but are you willing to live with that? Is that who you want to be?

I know what Jay's answer was.

And that's why there are people all over the world who will know exactly what you mean if you smile, and tell them:

Live like Jay.

EPILOGUE

An entire season passed before I returned to Mavericks. When I did, it was because Jeff Clark had decided to give out an award in Jay's honor and he wanted me to give it away. I've given out the Jay Award every year since. It's given to one of the twenty-four surfers who are invited every year to compete in the annual Mavericks surf contest. Winning the overall contest doesn't mean you will win the Jay, because it's about more than surfing.

The Jay Award is given to surfers who exemplify Jaybird's spirit—people of good will who participate in their community and are ambassadors of surfing. To win the Jay, you have to be a very good athlete, and a truly good person.

If Jay had lived, the award would have been named for someone else, and Jay would have won it every year.

Jay lived, and people like him live, following some basic concepts that I've tried to lay out through the course of this story. Here they are again:

Have a vision.

No one can live out someone else's vision; it has to come from within you.

To become a capable, competent individual, learn from capable, competent individuals.

Some people will always tell you that what you are trying to accomplish is impossible; those people have no idea what they're talking about.

So much of life is just perspective. So change your perspective, look at things differently, and see what else there is to see.

Don't give less than it is right for you to give.

If you're having a bad day, catch a wave.

When you find yourself going to extremes, a good coach will pull you aside and ask, "What are we really trying to achieve here?"

It's always cool to be number one, to win, but if you're not improving on your own performance, winning is negated.

As you become better than your friends, there begins to be an invisible wall, a little separation.

You have to break down every goal into smaller, achievable steps, and acknowledge accomplishing each of them.

You can only compete against yourself.

In sports, if you get inside someone's head, you own them. But it works both ways.

There's a focal point. There's something that you're actually supposed to be doing. If you get distracted for whatever reason, if you lose focus, then you're not going to be successful.

Take a moment to catch your breath and see what's really going on.

The more observant you are, over time you begin to build up a real understanding.

If you're thinking, you're already behind. You have to pre-think and prepare everything ahead of time.

With a lot of work, you can have an actual athletic experience through the process of visualization.

You need a strong data bank of information to draw from, but you can't just listen and not do.

When you're experimenting and trying to learn, you're going to fall— when you stop falling, you start stagnating.

For success, no matter what sport you're doing, start with something familiar.

Potential doesn't mean much if you don't put in the mental and physical work that is required to fulfill it.

You need to understand who you are, what you do that's good, and then try to figure out how best to display your strongest maneuvers and skills.

You have to be as informed as you can be about the situation ahead, but the only part of it you can actually control is yourself.

Your peace comes from knowing you've done all the things that you could have done. That's why you don't shortcut your training.

You can't deal with the storm when it's at its most tempestuous—you have to wait, and that takes a lot of resolve.

Make your agreements before you become emotionally involved, because you don't make good decisions when you're emotionally involved.

Work with what you're being given.

Either you are who you live to be, or you are not.

The better you become at something, if you're observant, you can see how many more things you could have done to make your performance even better.

We need to give young people the opportunity to do things that are larger than what they can envision.

In most situations, you can change. You can move. *You can do something to improve yourself and your situation. You have to be flexible. Your success can only come if you prepare yourself and have the ability to adapt. That comes about by being willing to invest in yourself and accept who you are today while being willing to morph into something better tomorrow.*

If people didn't pass along what they've learned, we would never progress.

It's easy to make a good athlete. It's very hard to make a good human being.

To be successful, you cannot let yourself be tainted by other people's fears.